GET GUERRILLA GARDENING

GET
GUERRILLA
GARDENING

ELLEN
MILES

A HANDBOOK FOR PLANTING IN PUBLIC PLACES

CONTENTS

HOW I GOT HERE

LIKE MANY GUERRILLA GARDENERS, I STARTED OUT NOT REALLY KNOWING WHAT I WAS DOING. OKAY, I DIDN'T KNOW WHAT I WAS DOING *AT ALL*...

Flash back to 2020. I'd just started Nature is a Human Right, a campaign for the United Nations to recognise access to healthy, green environments as a human right – a reaction to the inequalities highlighted (and exacerbated) at the time. It's a goal I stand by, but a long-term, top-down approach.

I wanted to do something more immediate, more tangible. So I reached out to local authorities, hoping they'd back some nimble greening in neglected spaces. I should've known better.

At the time, I was working in a London council myself, supporting a community organising project in one of the city's most nature-deprived wards. The passionate, knowledgeable, capable people in that community knew what their neighbourhoods needed, and how to make it happen. Still, the council wouldn't hand over the resources or rights to let them do that changemaking.

I had a lot of questions. Why was our work conducted in an ivory tower, miles away from the people we were meant to be working for? Why were we playing pass-the-paperwork when there was action to be taken? Why was more time and money spent on "impact measurement" than actual impact? The response was always the same: "That's just how things are done."

So I shouldn't have been surprised when my own council wasn't eager to let me loose on my postcode with a tubful of shrubs and a fistful of seeds. Instead, my query was tossed from one inbox to another, a hot potato in the "CC" field; any gaps in this virtual chain-link fence led to a thornbush of liability concerns and planning applications, snagging against action.

Around that time, a friend told me about "tactical urbanism", a movement he'd been active in back home in Buenos Aires, Argentina. Flicking through photos of painted streets and DIY street furniture, he explained that this "guerrilla" form of urban design happens when residents take ownership of their shared environment, carrying out low-cost interventions that reimagine wasted public space for public good.

Deep-diving into the idea, I came across the movement's green arm: guerrilla gardening. Cue LIGHTBULB MOMENT. *This was the answer! But...* The bulb shattered under a concrete question mark. *How do I do it?*

Now, when I say I had no idea what I was doing, *I had no idea what I was doing*. I wasn't a gardener. I'd never planted, pruned, or propagated. I hadn't sown a seed since Petri dish cress at school (and I'm pretty sure those didn't make it far). I needed help.

Guided by a belief in people power, I posted in three local groups (Nextdoor.co.uk, a mutual aid WhatsApp, and an eco-activism Facebook page) asking if anyone would like to join a guerrilla gardening community. Dozens of people replied with an enthusiastic "Yes!" I added everyone to a group chat, which was instantly buzzing with ideas. People hatched plans, swapped plants, shared advice, and turned dreams to schemes. Whoever could make it assembled on Sunday mornings, rain or shine, to plant whatever the season permitted. Buoyed by this lively ecosystem, I soon found my feet.

On a hunch that others might have the lightbulb moment I did, I started posting some of my guerrilla gardening efforts on TikTok. My second video (a seed bomb recipe) went viral, catapulting guerrilla gardening into a new generation's consciousness. As I kept posting, and millions stopped to watch, I realised there was a vast, latent army of green guerrillas out there – a youthwave with the potential to reverse global greyification. I was overjoyed! But they were apprehensive, asking the same thing I had: "How do I do it?"

So, I've spent the last three years working to a place where I can confidently answer that question, and give others a leg up. I've chatted to dozens of other botanical anarchists, acquired some qualifications, invested time in trowel and error, and founded Dream Green – a social enterprise that gets people guerrilla gardening with grants, guidance, and workshops.

Finally, I felt able to create the manual I wish had existed when I was getting started. This is it. And I have a feeling my journey only really begins here, with all of you.

WHAT IS GUERRILLA GARDENING?

GUERRILLA GARDENING IS GROWING PLANTS IN PUBLIC PLACES, IN RADICALLY GRASSROOTS FASHION.

GROWING PLANTS

Guerrilla gardening is about *growing*: adding to (not detracting from) the local ecosystem. How you do that is up to you! Whether you scatter native wildflower seeds onto a road verge, plant spring bulbs into a street tree bed, or turn a vacant lot into a community allotment, the aim is to transform the landscape from balding to bountiful. Unnecessary "weeding", crop sabotage, and plant theft don't cut the mustard.

PUBLIC PLACES

Cultivating your own private yard (or someone else's) isn't guerrilla gardening – even if you're using seed bombs and repurposed pallets. From wide open squares to hidden back alleys, guerrilla gardeners plant in shared spaces, bringing nature to the heart of neighbourhoods in ways that can benefit all residents, including local wildlife.

RADICALLY GRASSROOTS

Growing plants in a public place isn't always guerrilla gardening. The payrolled gardener tending your local park isn't a guerrilla gardener; a council-run community garden isn't a guerrilla garden. Why? The local authority has its finger in the pie, and can influence how (or even if) the garden grows.

The "guerrilla" aspect comes from being truly grassroots: growing entirely from the ground up, without municipal influence or involvement.

ALL ABOUT ACTION

Although it's a global movement, there's no one official guerrilla gardening group, association, or network. Many "guerrilla gardeners" haven't even heard the term! To become a bona fide guerrilla gardener, there's nothing to sign or subscribe to - you just need to take action, transforming a neglected scrap of public space into a vibrant pocket of plant life.

This means not going out of your way (or waiting around) for civic permission. Although every guerrilla garden is unique, one thing never changes: guerrilla gardening unites flower power and people power.

AND WHAT IS IT NOT?

GROWING ON LAND THAT "ISN'T YOURS"

Guerrilla gardening is often framed as gardening on land that isn't yours. But ownership has dimensions beyond financial purchase. The perspective that land is an economic commodity is blinkered and dangerous (it has displaced Indigenous people and marginalised urban communities from places they've called home for generations).

Land was once a community resource – collectively managed by all, for the good of all. Today, most public places fail to serve the public: commerce and cars reign over community welfare; land is wasted and neglected under state control.

Given that our habitats impact our health and happiness, and are a front line of the unfolding climate crisis, it's our right – our responsibility even – to make them work for people and planet. Guerrilla gardeners do just this, by "using plants to reclaim public space for the public good".

By actively engaging with the land in ways that give back – to the land itself and to all its residents, human and non-human – I believe ownership (and land rights) can be earned, not bought.

GARDENING ILLEGALLY

Defining guerrilla gardening as "illegal gardening" is lazy and misleading. For starters, various outlawed forms of gardening (like marijuana farms) are not guerrilla gardening. What's more, guerrilla gardening isn't necessarily illegal...

WHOSE LAND IS IT ANYWAY?

» Is our shared earth really just a financial asset, to be portioned off and parcelled up for the highest bidder?
» If the places people live, work, play, participate, breathe, and grow aren't theirs, whose are they?
» Can land ever "belong" to a corporate entity, or a cash-rich interloper, more than to the people who belong to it?

IS GUERRILLA GARDENING ILLEGAL?

THERE'S NO CLEAR ANSWER TO THIS. THE LEGALITIES OF GRASSROOTS GREENING ARE, IRONICALLY, A GREY AREA.

Some places let you plant (almost) anywhere: Paris offers citizens a "permis de végétaliser", a licence to plant that "allows everyone to garden in public space". However, this isn't an automatic right; you have to apply for permission for each project, as a group of five or more. Some places let you plant without permission: Los Angeles allows residents to plant, *without* a permit, in the parkways directly outside their houses. However, this right doesn't extend beyond that thin strip, or beyond their list of "approved" species.

Nowhere, it seems, are the two – plant anywhere, without first seeking permission – combined:

I'm not aware of a single law that clearly states that citizens can (or can't) autonomously grow on any scrap of public soil. That said, I'm not omniscient, so check what your local policies are (though be wary, they may well be vague or near-impossible to pin down).

Confusing things further, authorities' official stances often don't match up to their actions. The San Francisco Department of Public Works classifies guerrilla grafting (pages 42–43) as vandalism but, since 2012, the municipality has not actively pursued grafters. On the flipside, East London's Hackney council took a public stance of allowing residents to plant in tree beds in 2021, but then "weeded" people's careful planting out in 2022, turning dozens of little green oases into parched dirt deserts.

The good news is, in the absence of laws specific to it, guerrilla gardening isn't *inherently* illegal. The less good news is, there are still various related charges that authorities could use against you (though they probably won't). Here's a run-down of the main areas of law that could potentially land you in trouble, and how you can best avoid them:

YOU COULD ARGUE VANDALISM IS A MATTER OF PERSPECTIVE

Graffiti artist Banksy's work ceased to be "vandalism" years ago and can now shoot a property's value up by over 1,000%. It seems even more nonsensical to call an urban garden - a beautiful thing and a public health resource, where before there was only dereliction - "damaging" (especially since it's not classed as criminal damage when the council cuts down a tree or paves over soil). To be on the safe side though, it's best to not rely on winning a philosophical debate about the subjective nature of aesthetics.

CRIMINAL DAMAGE

What it is: Vandalism. Damaging or defacing property that doesn't belong to you.

How to avoid it: Avoid causing any permanent physical changes to public property, including pavements, walls, and street furniture. Make sure that anything you build (planters, seats, signs, and so on) can be removed without a trace and don't grow plants with roots or vines that could cause structural damage, like English ivy (*Hedera helix*).

TRESPASS

What it is: Entering private land or property without permission.

How to avoid it: Only plant on public land, not private property. This approach not only makes you exempt from trespassing, it also means other people can benefit from your planting.

PUBLIC NUISANCE

What it is: Action that causes a nuisance to others, like making them feel uncomfortable or stopping them from going about their daily business.

How to avoid it: Be considerate of others. In particular, take care not to block off the path of wheelchairs, mobility scooters, or prams, and keep mess and noise to a minimum.

PUBLIC ENDANGERMENT

What it is: Reckless behaviour that is likely to harm other people.

How to avoid it: This isn't very sexy, but put health and safety first. This means sanding wood down, keeping paths clear to avoid trip hazards and obstructions, making sure your built structures aren't going to fall apart, and not growing anything toxic to the touch, such as monk's hood (*Aconitum napellus*).

PLANTING INVASIVE SPECIES

What it is: Some species that aren't native to your area can take over, endangering the local ecosystem. Most places have laws against cultivating these plants (particularly outside private gardens).

How to avoid it: Wherever you live in the world, research what's invasive in your area and avoid it. To be even safer, research what's native and stick to planting those species (pages 103 and 174).

GUERRILLA GARDENING CAN ACTUALLY REDUCE CRIME: PROJECTS TO "GREEN" SCRAP LAND HAVE LED TO DROPS IN GUN VIOLENCE, VANDALISM, AND BURGLARIES.

GARDENERS VS THE LAW

Three headline-grabbing cases of guerrilla gardeners who fought the law. (Spoiler alert: they all win).

2008. London, England

The Metropolitan Police threaten to take Richard Reynolds into custody for "criminal damage" after spotting him and others planting purple flowers under a roadside chevron sign. The group avoid charges by agreeing to leave, but return two hours later and finish the job unscathed.

2010. Los Angeles, USA

City authorities take offence to the fresh fruit and vegetables growing on a road verge, citing a law that sidewalks and curbs must be "free of obstruction". The man behind them, fashion designer Ron Finley, is told he must remove the plants, or pay $400 for a permit. After asserting his right not to do either, Ron receives a warrant for his arrest. He starts a campaign, which gets picked up by major global media. The publicly shamed LA City Council not only backs down, they change the law: now, Angelenos can plant (approved species) in their nearest parkway without a permit.

2021. Pretoria, South Africa

The City of Tshwane issues a fine to Djo BaNkuna for "interfering with municipal infrastructure" by planting brassicas in bare streetside soil. "The Cabbage Bandit" refuses to pay the fine, goes to court (representing himself), and wins. At his manifesto launch, President Cyril Ramaphosa promises to "ensure the unrestricted development of urban and pavement gardens where crops can be planted to increase food security."

The moral of these stories? Green-thumbed "offenders" can win out over red-faced authorities. Today, it's getting even easier to argue our case. There's growing public support for green cities and community-led change, and waning tolerance for regulations designed to protect profits and power structures over people.

STAY VIGILANT, VIGILANTE

So, these are the realities and potential pitfalls. While you might be stopped and questioned by authorities, it's unlikely you'll be convicted. A 2022 report in the international journal *Crime, Media, Culture* described guerrilla gardening as "a form of urban intervention that is broadly accepted and welcomed, *even by those who enforce the law.*" That said, it'd be irresponsible of me to claim that there's *no chance* of a brush with the forces. Check the latest laws where you live (as best you can) and stay vigilant.

A NOTE ON PRIVILEGE

GUERRILLA GARDENING IS FOR EVERYONE.

Unfortunately, our criminal "justice" systems don't have a similar equal opportunities track record. It would be remiss not to acknowledge the role that background, income, and ethnicity play in how police treat people. I don't think it's a coincidence that two of the men in these (rare) clashes with the law - the two who were actually charged - are Black. On the other hand, I expect being a white, middle class, cis woman has contributed to the fact I've never been so much as questioned.

To others of you with such privileges, practise effective allyship. Take one for the team and nominate yourself as the designated spokesperson for your guerrilla gardening group if the police do show up, taking the heat off those from persecuted and minoritised demographics (pages 170-171).

And to absolutely everyone reading this, make sure you know your rights! (Pages 167 and 175)

WINNING THE RIGHT TO GROW

Guerrilla gardening is as much about greening this metaphorical "grey area" of legalities as it is greening literal grey areas of towns and cities. Despite what the media might say about guerrilla gardeners, we don't just want to "break the rules" – we want to end them. We envisage a world free from authoritarian restrictions on who has a right to grow, in which public spaces are treated as commons, and everyone is allowed (and encouraged) to participate in shaping their environment.

How do we realise this future? Direct action. This includes shifting from covert to overt: planting in broad daylight, and talking to anyone who wants to know what we're up to. Plus, recognising that rights and responsibilities go hand in hand. We have a responsibility to guerrilla garden competently, safely, and impactfully, in ways that boost public wellbeing and the environment, and lighten the load for public services rather than increase it!

By acting like we already have a right to grow, guerrilla gardeners show what could be possible if we did, and provide a blueprint for a society in which it's normal to see citizens taking responsibility for public spaces and local nature.

For real change to happen, policymakers must be – as Incredible Edible co-founder Mary Clear says – "the other hand clapping" along with grassroots action. Rather than clipping our wings, the state should be the wind beneath them. So, while the powers that be fail to act in our best interests, it's our right to fail to comply with their rules.

"ENVISAGING A FUTURE IN WHICH ALL SPECIES CAN FLOURISH IS ALL ABOUT POSSIBILITIES, NOT CONSTRAINTS."

Caroline Till & Kate Franklin

> ## "DIRECT ACTION IS, ULTIMATELY, THE DEFIANT INSISTENCE ON ACTING AS IF ONE IS ALREADY FREE."
> **David Graeber**

LEGITIMISATION IS NOT THE ENEMY

The most successful guerrilla gardens often become "legitimised" by local authorities: Liz Christy's Bowery Houston community garden, Richard Reynolds' tower block bed, Ron Finley's parkway, and Hackney's Garden of Earthly Delights all won their respective council's recognition. Legitimisation is not the enemy of the guerrilla gardener - ridiculous restrictions are!

A POTTED HISTORY

HISTORIES OF GUERRILLA GARDENING ARE LIKE CHICKEN WIRE: MORE HOLES THAN MATERIAL.

Why? It's likely most guerrilla gardens are created out of necessity by people pushed to the fringes of society – the homeless, nationless, and moneyless – who keep these lifelines hidden to ensure their survival.

The contemporary cases we *do* know about point to a deep-rooted tradition: the greens grown along train tracks in Mumbai; crop fields cultivated by landless Kenyan farmers; Brazil's co-created and self-managed favela gardens; and food and flowers tended by Syrians in the Domiz refugee camp are more likely instances of history repeating itself than historical anomalies.

So remember, although the following timeline takes place on a Western backdrop, this is more reflective of the way history is written than the movement's true, but hidden, story.

IN THE BEGINNING

Although we can't know exactly when or where the first act of guerrilla gardening took place, we *can* identify the earliest possible points it could have emerged by looking at land rights. In places and times where land was treated as a common resource, and all growing was community-led and in shared spaces, the concept of "guerrilla gardening" would be meaningless. The first act(s) of guerrilla gardening can only have happened after land was colonised, privatized, and commodified. Indeed, two of the earliest recorded examples of guerrilla gardening are a direct response to such events...

"WE WILL NEVER KNOW THE NAME OF THE WORLD'S FIRST GUERRILLA GARDENER."
David Tracey

AFRICAN FARMERS

THE AMERICAS, 1500S–1800S

As European forces colonised large parts of the African continent, enslaved farmers ingeniously braided seeds into their hair to retain autonomy, food security, and a connection to the homes they were torn from. Landing in the Americas, these experts grew in abundance on their oppressors' land (itself violently taken from Indigenous communities).

In contrast to their forced land work, these secret gardens were a form of resistance, survival, and sovereignty. As scholar Geri Augusto says:

> "Enslaved people took the initiative... to create small plots and provision grounds... either beside the slave hut or... [on] a piece of land that the plantation owner didn't need... [T]hey would raise vegetables, medicinal plants, and even flowers... They were supplementing their diet, but also it was a small, small patch in which they could be human."

As their crops flourished, these brave and bright growers became responsible for the successful presence of rice, watermelon, coffee, kola, yams, and many other species grown in the Americas today.

CULTIVATING IN CAPTIVITY

There's a bittersweet tendency for people in captivity to cultivate the spaces that confine them. In Guantanamo Bay - a detention camp synonymous with injustice and human rights violations - detainees kept seeds from meals, along with plastic spoons to use as trowels.

1960S & 1970S USA

'60s and '70s USA saw a wave of countercultural (r)evolution and political idealism. It was a time of love and fear, as visions of peace and unity drifted over a reality of neo-colonial war and police brutality. Martin Luther King Jr dreamed and John Lennon imagined, as Black Power radicals founded schools and farming co-operatives, and hippies staged love-ins for peace and nature. This radical zeitgeist supported the first seeds of activity that would later blossom into "guerrilla gardening" as we now know it.

THE DIGGERS

SURREY, ENGLAND, 1649

Before this overseas expansion, England's ruling classes had colonised their own nation. As right to roam activist and author Nick Hayes says, "it's like we practised seizing land and exploiting labour on our own soil before we exported it to other nations."

Starting in the 12th century, and picking up pace between 1450 and 1640, the British aristocracy had gone around enclosing (i.e. stealing) *commons*, parcels of land that regular folk (known as "commoners") relied on for food, fuel, and other essential resources. In response to the resulting cost of living and malnutrition crises, a group of radicals, now known as The Diggers, began planting vegetables on a hillside. Their aim was to restore the land as "a Common Treasury for All... That every one that is born in the land, may be fed by the Earth".

They probably weren't the first group to cultivate a former commons. However, somewhat surprisingly, the Diggers didn't try to hide what they were doing. Quite the opposite: the group's leader, Gerrard Winstanley, published reams of campaigning papers. While this succeeded in securing their place in the history books, it also attracted scrutiny. The result? Their camp didn't even last the summer. The landlord drove them out, accusing the peaceful group of illegal assembly, riot, and trespass.

PEOPLE'S PARK
CALIFORNIA, 1969

The University of California had run out of cash while developing a 2.8-acre site into student facilities – leaving the block a muddy, messy nothing. One Sunday, hundreds of locals responded to a call to take over the space and began planting trees, grass, and flowers in the upturned soil. More than a square of turf and a poetry stand, the new "People's Park" embodied the social values of the politically disillusioned Vietnam generation.

Appalled, the university ordered authorities to rip out every root and erect a fence around the space. Thousands of people turned up to defend the park. Ronald Reagan, then state governor, made his stance towards demonstrators clear: "If there has to be a bloodbath, let's get it over with". In the carnage that came to be known as "Bloody Thursday", police shot at the demonstrators, killing one person and harming scores more.

More protests followed over the next 50 years. At the time of writing, although People's Park still exists (and was nationally recognised as a Historic Place in 2022), it's under serious threat from the university's development plans.

Adam Purple's "Garden of Eden", Eldridge Street, New York City (1985).

NYC GARDENS
NEW YORK, 1970S

The early 1970s financial crisis led to around 25,000 litter-filled, rat-infested vacant lots across America's "City of Dreams". These magnets for crime and disease might have seemed an unlikely place to start a garden, but the city's visionaries – including artists, students, and Puerto Rican communities – saw otherwise.

Perhaps the best known of these visionaries was artist Liz Christy, who set out to reclaim life and land in the East Village with her group the "Green Guerillas" – so coining the phrase "guer(r)illa gardening". The squad started by throwing seed bombs over fences and greening tree beds. With these successes, their ambitions grew, and they took over a vast space at the junction of Bowery and Houston. Though Liz tragically died aged just 39, this garden (renamed in her honour) still exists today.

A 10-minute walk away, from 1975–1986, you'd have found the Garden of Eden, which filled an entire barren block on Eldridge Street. Guerrilla Adam Purple brought in horse manure, scooped off the Central Park paving, along with his own "humanure", to fertilise flowering trees, fruit-bearing bushes, and fresh herbs and vegetables. "The city was doing nothing about the land, they were abusing it", he complained. "It's the people's turf. I made that garden for everybody".

GUERRILLAGARDENING. ORG

ENGLAND, 2000s

In 2004, green-fingered ad man Richard Reynolds started cultivating a neglected council flower bed outside his tower block. An avid gardener without a yard of his own, Reynolds said, "It came to me that my need to garden could be satisfied through... public beds". He started a blog, GuerrillaGardening. org, to document his exploits, and news of it spread like wildflowers.

He added a forum to the site, and called it "The global hub for... guerrilla gardeners". This unifying vision helped thousands of guerrilla gardeners around the world to connect, and skyrocketed the movement's visibility. Some, though, questioned the fact that site users had to "enlist" as Reynolds' "troops", sensing it as monopolisation by a "self-appointed general".

Even so, no one could deny Reynolds' impact on the field. His tenacious advocacy for guerrilla gardening and influential book, *On Guerrilla Gardening* (2008), inspired countless people (including several I've met) to start planting in public places. And, though the GuerrillaGardening.org forum no longer exists, its legacy lives on in illicit gardens across the planet.

TODAY

Today, eminent figures in the guerrilla gardening movement are focused on hyperlocal action, empowering communities, and supporting our living planet. Many of us seek to come full circle, to recover a world in which the concept of "guerrilla gardening" can again become meaningless because all land is treated as collectively managed common ground.

NOW IT'S YOUR TIME

If you ever feel alone when out "in the field" (which for us means out on the street), just remember you're part of a global, ancient community of freedom seeders.

SAGE ADVICE

THE SEASONED GUERRILLA GARDENERS
I'VE SPOKEN TO ECHO THREE KEY PIECES
OF ADVICE:

START SMALL

Don't set yourself up for disappointment by biting off more than you can chew. Start small and build up to bigger projects as your confidence, connections, and abilities grow.

> **"I DIDN'T START HOSTING EVENTS WITH 30 VOLUNTEERS RIGHT AWAY. I STARTED BY PUTTING SEEDS ON AN EMPTY STREET TREE BED, UNSURE IF ANYTHING WOULD GROW."**
> **Simone Marques, Green & Blue Eco Care**

JUST DO IT

You can't predict how things will go until you actually get going. So, get going! And welcome any "failures" as a necessary part of the learning process. Just ensure you're not planting anything harmful (pages 13 and 103).

"Don't worry about making mistakes – just figure it out as you go. It's not rocket science, there's a good chance things will work out!"
– Alan Hurley, Mad About Cork

RESIST & PERSIST

Guerrilla gardening takes grit. From combative busybodies and authorities, to blight and drought, we face challenges from all sides and must stay resilient in the face of them. It's our responsibility to be tenacious and care for the gardens we create.

"Guerrilla gardening is about sustainable change, not making more work for low-paid council labourers when we've lost interest."
– John Welsh, Rewilding the City

C.L.A.S.H CULTURE

THESE PRINCIPLES ARE THE FERTILE SOIL FROM WHICH CONSIDERATE GUERRILLA GARDENING GROWS.

COMMIT TO CARE
A guerrilla garden is not just for spring! Become your site's gardening angel, ensuring it's watered, protected, litter free, and nourished.

LET NATURE LEAD
Work with nature, not against it. Reject chemical pesticides, embrace undervalued life forms (from weeds to woodlice), go organic, and prioritise native species.

ACT LOCAL
Grow where you've put down your own roots. Other people's neighbourhoods are theirs to shape (though you can support them).

SEEK SUSTAINABILITY
Be eco-minded. Borrow and repurpose instead of buying new, use peat-free compost, and source plants and parts as locally and responsibly as possible.

HAVE FUN!
The reasons we guerrilla garden might be serious, but doing it doesn't have to be. Centre joy, celebrate small wins, and see challenges as opportunities to get creative.

THE 7 Ps

Guerrilla gardening doesn't have to be complicated or time-consuming. You can grab a handful of seeds and scatter them in your wake. Job done.

On the other hand, a universe of possibilities can open up once you know all the angles you can consider. So, if you want to dig deeper, read on

Here's my "7 Ps" framework for creating a guerrilla garden:.

PURPOSE
Know your purpose

PLACE
Find a place

PEOPLE
Gather people

PLAN
Craft a plan

PARTS
Get the parts

PLANTING
Do the planting

PROTECT
Provide and protect

THIS IS A GUIDEBOOK, NOT A RULEBOOK

Although this is generally a smart order to act in, you may want to flip some of the steps around (depending on your circumstances). You might find an amazing site before you know what local needs it can address, or be given a bunch of plants before you know where they'll go. Usually, it isn't linear: you'll circle back to planning, recruiting, planting, and so on as the project evolves.

PURPOSE — PURPOSE — PURPOSE

KNOW YOUR PURPOSE

THIS IS NO TIME TO BE A REBEL WITHOUT A CAUSE. THE WORLD NEEDS AN ARMY OF REBELS *WITH* A CAUSE.

The first step in creating a guerrilla garden is to know why you're doing it. This sets you up for all the decisions that follow. You might want to make a big political statement about the recommoning of public land, you might simply want to spruce up a sad street corner. Both are equally valid.

Though it would be impossible to cover every reason to create a pocket paradise (each guerrilla garden is personal and niche to its neighbourhood), this chapter offers a bouquet of examples.

FIRST, LOOK INWARD

Before deciding on your garden's purpose (the impact you want it to have), consider your own motivations, and what you stand to gain by becoming a guerrilla gardener. Be honest with yourself; knowing what drives you can keep you going when you run into hurdles.

WHAT DO YOU LOVE?
PEOPLE Exposure to green, leafy environments is a pillar of our health and happiness, but access to these spaces often falls along the fault lines of income and ethnicity. Many guerrilla gardeners fight for social justice by bringing beautiful biodiversity to the postcodes, blocks, and streets that need it most.

Did you join a mutual aid group during lockdown? Perhaps you

volunteer in the community? If you're into helping the people around you, you might decide to create a guerrilla garden as a public health resource, a way to improve local people's mood and mindset, or to empower and connect the community.

Guerrilla gardens boost people's wellbeing by redressing unequal access to nature

» Proximity to quality nature is linked to better mental health, IQ, temperament, immune resilience, life expectancy, and much more.
» Around 1 in 3 people in England do not have access to nature near home.
» 100 million people in the USA live further than 10 minutes' walk from a park.

PLANTS You might plant a guerrilla garden simply because you love growing things! If you lack a garden or allotment of your own, you can create one on bare, wasted land.

Even if you do have outside space, you might be curious about taking your skills beyond the confines of your private garden to splash colour and life into the nooks and crannies of your neighbourhood.

WHY GUERRILLA GARDEN?

At the risk of sounding like a star-spangled bumper sticker: it's about freedom and justice. I believe we have a right to engage with the land we live on, and a responsibility to, too. Our governments have shown they can't be trusted to act in the best interests of people or the planet. Resilient regeneration has to grow from the ground up. It's up to us to create the bright future we deserve, with stubborn optimism, creativity, and courage.

GUERRILLA GARDENS CAN PROVIDE...

» Wildlife habitats
» Community spaces
» Joy and stress relief
» Fresh food
» Beauty and colour
» Cleaner, cooler streets
» A political statement

... often all at once.

Do you love plants but lack land? You're not alone:

» There are 37 billion acres of land on Earth – that's enough, in theory, for everyone to have 4.5 acres (3 football pitches). Instead, a handful of people own far more than a fair share: Queen Elizabeth II owned 6.6 billion acres (that's almost one-sixth of *all land on the planet*); the Pope owns 177 million acres.

» Half of England is owned by less than 1% of its population.

» Black people in England are nearly 4 times as likely as white people to have no access to outdoor space at home.

PLANET We're facing the greatest crisis in the history of humanity. But the looming threat of climate collapse often feels abstract and impossibly complex – so much so that we question our ability to make a difference. It's easy to feel like the best we can do is to simply limit our negative impact rather than increase our positive influence. In other words, climate "action" usually seems to be a case of *in*action: not taking flights, not buying fast fashion, not eating meat... It's a lot of *not*.

Guerrilla gardening, on the other hand, is fun, creative climate action, with visible, tangible impact. It's a "nature-based solution" to environmental unravelling: it helps nature by mobilising nature's "technology".

Guerrilla gardens can counter...

» **Air pollution** by capturing particulate matter and converting carbon dioxide into oxygen.

» **Heat waves** by providing shade, increasing evapotranspiration, and through the low thermal mass and solar reflectance of soil and leaves (compared to hard surfacing).

» **Biodiversity loss** by bringing plants to nature-deprived areas, and by creating habitats and shelter for wildlife.

Guerrilla gardens not only address these symptoms of climate change, but also one of its key causes: the disconnect between humans and (the rest of) nature.

HOPE It's easy to be a cynic. We're in a time of unprecedented crises, in health, community, and ecology... and the people in power can't be relied on to do anything about it. No one would blame you for feeling powerless. But you're not. And guerrilla gardening proves it: it's a way you can make the world a better place with your own two hands. Hope will flourish out of persistent action and its inevitable results.

PRIDE By guerrilla gardening, you have the power to enact social and environmental justice in one fell dig. You can grow a network of green havens, creating and connecting wildlife habitats while supporting human minds, bodies, and communities. You can help reimagine your city, and your role within it. You will be part of the change the world needs and on the right side of history.

WHAT DO YOU WANT?

As well as all the usual benefits from gardening (serenity, purpose, nature connection, and, of course, food and flowers), guerrilla gardeners stand to gain even more:

BELONGING We're taught to pass through our neighbourhoods as if we don't belong to them, and they to us. But when we help shape these places we can truly feel we belong. By taking an active role in shaping your surroundings, rather than drifting through them in resigned acceptance, you'll forge transformative relationships with places and people.

THEN, LOOK FORWARD

The next step is to consider the impact you want your garden to have in the world. Read on for some common guerrilla gardening goals, from supporting biodiversity to protest.

SUPPORT BIODIVERSITY

Biodiversity, the variety of living species in an ecosystem, is the foundation of a liveable world. Without diversity of flora, fauna, fungi, and microscopic organisms, we wouldn't have breathable air, edible food, or potable water.

You'd think this would be enough reason to respect and protect delicately balanced biomes – not to mention living beings' inherent value. Instead, human destruction of wild habitats is causing the sixth mass extinction: wiping out species on Earth at 100 to 1,000 times the natural rate. We are burning the library of life, killing off untold species before we even know they exist, or learn of the links they provide in their ecosystem's fragile chain.

Many guerrilla gardeners set out to push back against this terrifying trend. By bringing native greenery to grey areas, acts of guerrilla rewilding restore plant diversity, rebuild broken links in the local ecosystem, and provide essential food and shelter for wildlife.

WHY IT MATTERS

» The UK has lost nearly half its biodiversity since the Industrial Revolution.
» One-third of wildlife in the USA is at risk of extinction.
» It's estimated that dozens of species go extinct every day, with as many as 30-50% of all species on Earth going extinct by 2050.

HUMAN DESTRUCTION
OF WILD HABITATS IS
CAUSING THE SIXTH
MASS EXTINCTION:
WIPING OUT SPECIES
ON EARTH AT 100 TO
1,000 TIMES THE
NATURAL RATE.

@SFINBLOOM

Mission District, San Francisco

When filmmaker Shalaco found an old parmesan shaker in a thrift shop, rather than overlooking it, he saw something else.

He filled the vessel with native wildflower seeds and rice hulls and gifted "the mega-epic seed shaker" to landscape designer Phoenix. Before long, they'd turned grungy local streets into life-lit eco-corridors, teeming with native wildflowers and pollinators.

In April 2021, the couple decided to combine their skills to show how easy – and fun – supporting local biodiversity can be. They started filming their seed-shaking mini-missions, or as they call it "volunteer urban conservation", around San Francisco's Mission District. Project @SFinBloom became an instant TikTok sensation, and it's easy to see why. Far from the stereotypical conservationist's clipboards and microchips, Shalaco and Phoenix equip themselves with seed-filled

"NORMALISE PLANTING NATIVE WILDFLOWERS."

Shalaco & Phoenix

toy guns and motorised skateboards.

Behind this whimsical approach is a serious mission. "One in four native bees in North America are endangered," Phoenix tells me, as we sit in their plant-packed sitting-room-come-studio. "Sightings of the western monarch butterfly have dropped 99.9% since the 80s. Supporting biodiversity is more important now than ever before – so we try to make it more accessible and approachable. The shakers and seed guns take conservation off a pedestal and help to democratise it."

And it's working. The "hipster horticulturalists" have reached millions of people around the world with their idiosyncratic approach to guerrilla gardening and catchy call to action: Normalise planting native wildflowers. "We're in awe of the hundreds of thousands of people who've responsibly spread native wildflower seeds throughout their neighbourhoods," Shalaco raves, wearing a t-shirt that says B.D.S.M (Bees Do So Much). "You can change the world!"

MAKE A SEED SHAKER

Follow in @SFinBloom's footsteps to leave your own floral footprint around town.

GET EQUIPPED

Cheese or salt shaker

Organic rice hulls or
  buckwheat husks

Native wildflower
  seeds

Scissors

Scrap of fabric

Rubber band

01.

Find a parmesan cheese shaker or diner-style salt shaker – ideally get one second hand.

02.

Fill it with organic rice hulls or buckwheat husks. These will help space out the seeds as they are sown, so that they don't overcrowd the area and compete for resources.

WAKE & SHAKE

03.

Pour in the native wildflower seeds, filling in the gaps between the husks. Shake the vessel gently to disperse the seeds all the way through.

04.

Cut a scrap of fabric to cover the top (to stop the seeds escaping) and seal it with a rubber band.

Carry your shaker with you wherever you go and scatter native seeds onto any bare soil you pass. If you can, water them in to give the seeds a helping start.

CREATE BEAUTY

On the surface, choosing "beautification" as your purpose may sound, well, superficial. But seeing beauty around us, compared to desolation or dereliction, has real impact. "Beautiful environments," Dr Samantha Walton, author of *Everybody Needs Beauty* (2021), tells me, "lift people's spirits, calm and comfort us, and leave us feeling happier and healthier. Beauty helps us feel pride in our area, which translates to a sense of dignity."

This doesn't mean we should just be thoughtlessly led by subjective beauty standards. As Dr Walton warns, "Sometimes we need to challenge ideas of what is beautiful. The 18th century preference for flat lawns, for example. It's time we move on from that 'neat and tidy' paradigm and find beauty in weeds and wildness."

Fortunately, we do find untamed natural landscapes beautiful (even if we don't always realise it). Data scientist Dr Chanuki Illushka Seresinhe and her colleagues uncovered this preference by analysing 1.5 million ratings of various outdoor settings: "Plain grass wasn't so highly rated," she explains, "there's something about wilder nature that people are innately drawn to."

So, guerrilla gardening should aim for natural beauty by reintroducing biodiversity – not culling it. Dr Walton agrees: "I always think of guerrilla gardening as adding something in, not pulling something out. So much urban planning is about 'just enough' nature; the exciting potential of guerrilla gardening is to disrupt that blankness."

"BEAUTIFUL SIGHTS, BEAUTIFUL SMELLS, THAT SHOULD BE NORMAL, NOT ALL THIS BLIGHT, ALL THIS TRASH, ALL THIS DESOLATE, STINKY, CONCRETE, SMOG, HEAT."

Ron Finley

WHY IT MATTERS

- » According to renowned biologist E.O. Wilson, famed for his "biophilia hypothesis": "Nature holds the key to our aesthetic… satisfaction".
- » Looking at flourishing plant life can replenish energy, reduce stress, and restore focus.
- » People living in "very scenic" places are more likely to report "good" or "very good" health than residents of areas deemed "not scenic", even with socioeconomic disparities taken into account.

» 13.5 million households in the USA are in "food deserts" - areas in which access to fresh, nutritious food is either non-existent or extremely limited.

» In the UK, it costs twice as much to get 100 calories from fresh, single-ingredient food than from ultra-processed, readymade meals. As a consequence, 1 in 5 people's diet consists of 80% preservative-heavy, vitamin-low food.

» Research by UK charity The Food Foundation found that people on the lowest incomes would have to spend nearly 75% of their "disposable" income on food to achieve the government's healthy eating guidelines. In Northern Ireland, low income families would have to spend up to half (46%) of their entire weekly income on groceries to afford healthy food.

GROW FOOD

Tabloids sneer at mums serving microwave suppers. Reproachful glares shoot through neon-lit windows at teenagers in chicken shops. Policymakers point fingers (in the wrong direction), slapping calories on fast food menus and "fat tax" on fizzy drinks. Our society demonises poor nutrition without recognising it for what it is: not a moral failing, but a symptom of broken systems.

Food systems and policies – all too often influenced by corporations with a bias for profit over public health – make unhealthy food more accessible (and appealing) than healthy options. This has not only fed a rise in obesity and Type 2 diabetes among the poorest members of society but has also led to a state of widespread food insecurity across so-called "developed" countries.

No one should be hungry or struggle to access fresh food, and people should be able to feed their families without shame. Growing food in your neighbourhood can help alleviate dependence on multinationals and reframe fresh food as a social good – and a right – rather than a luxury. Local food production also means fewer "food miles", less packaging, and less chemical use, than industrial production.

Of course, you don't have to experience food insecurity to want to grow fresh herbs, fruit, and vegetables. But, if you are lucky enough to be in this position, consider who in your area could also benefit from your harvest.

GUERRILLA GRAFT

The fruit trees you'll find in cities are often ornamental trees, which can't actually bear fruit. Councils plant these to avoid having to deal with upkeep, and the "mess" of fallen fruit (as if people wouldn't eat it from the tree). By grafting a fruit-bearing branch, you can create a free, healthy food source for your neighbourhood.

GET EQUIPPED

Budding fruit-bearing tree

Sturdy, sharp knife (sterilized)

Labels

Pen

Airtight container

Ornamental fruit tree

Grafting tape

Rubber band

The best time to do this is early spring. Be careful while you're working, so you don't harm the tree – or yourself!

01.

Collect budding cuttings (called "scions") from a fruit-bearing tree in your area. If you're taking multiple cuttings, label with the plant variety, cutting date, and location. Store in the fridge in an airtight container with a sprinkle of water in it. They'll keep for a month.

02.

Find an ornamental street tree of the same fruit type you took your cutting from. Look for a branch (the "stock") the same width as your scion cutting. Use a sturdy, sharp knife to cut the end of the scion into a V-shaped wedge. Cut the stock flat, then cut a straight slit into it that is the same depth as the wedge's height (to ensure a tight fit).

04.

Holding the graft union together firmly, wrap it tightly in grafting tape, starting from below the graft and ending above it. You want pressure between the touching tissue edges to help them fuse. Secure the union with a rubber band.

05.

After a month, remove the rubber band. You may wish to label your graft with the date you did it.

vascular cambium

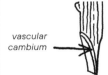

03.

Insert the scion. The scion's growth tissue ("vascular cambium") – the thin layer of green just below the bark, which transports water and sugar – must align with the stock's.

Check in on your graft regularly and water your tree to keep it healthy. Be patient; it takes 2–5 years for a grafted branch to bear fruit.

PROVIDE EDUCATION

In the words of the futurist educator Zak Stein: "If education is not the answer you are asking the wrong question." When it comes to building a greener, fairer future, I would add: "If education *in nature* is not the answer, you're asking the wrong question."

How can we foster an action-inspiring reverence for all life on Earth? Education in nature. How can we help communities be more self-sufficient and better connected? Education in nature. How can we raise a generation of leaders who shape regenerative systems? Ed... You get the point.

But interactive, in situ learning about nature is currently a privilege. Forget forest schools, many children learn in environments lacking vegetation entirely. Playgrounds are tarmacked over; nature, with its "dirt" and "germs", is kept a JCB-arm's length away. Ron Finley thinks there are other reasons for this: "Why don't they teach us we can plant a seed in the ground and grow a tree that gives you fruit and a thousand more seeds? (Talk about rate of return! That's power.) It's by design – it's not happenstance."

Guerrilla gardening can democratise nature education by creating spaces in which curious minds (of all ages!) can learn about the cycles of life and seasons, watch the give and take of ecosystems, experience the magic and wonder of nature, and learn how to work with it as a result. Could your guerrilla garden be a classroom, art studio, playground, or laboratory?

STRENGTHEN COMMUNITY

Humans are hardwired to need community. Strong social ties improve health, boost happiness, and provide a life-affirming sense of belonging. But capitalist urban planning and digital hyper-connection have eroded these links, and left us more socially and somatically disconnected than ever.

Perhaps surprisingly, loneliness is affecting young people more than older generations. In England, those aged 16–24 are the most likely to feel lonely "often" or "always", and the least likely to feel a strong sense of belonging to their neighbourhood. Alienation also maps onto marginalisation: disabled people are almost four times more likely than non-disabled people to experience persistent loneliness; racism, xenophobia, and other forms of discrimination trigger loneliness for many people subject to them; and over a third of homeless service users often feel isolated.

But there is hope. Public gardens bring people together. Grassroots action brings people together. So guerrilla gardening (which involves both) is fertile soil for social bonds to grow and flourish. Building (comm)unity through collaborative, purposeful guerrilla gardening can combat loneliness, empower marginalised members of your neighbourhood, and build collective resilience.

WHY IT MATTERS

» Urban nature sprouts kindness and connection. Studies have found that we're more likely to return a stranger's dropped glove, strike up a conversation with someone from another culture, and behave selflessly in green urban spaces compared to grey ones.

» All kinds of communities can benefit from guerrilla gardening and its results. In lockdown, a group of LGBTQ+ youth used the secluded Garden of Earthly Delights in Hackney as a safe outdoor space to meet up.

» Leicester-based horticulturalist Hafsah Hafeji tells me, "I've seen many people connect with their culture and heritage through growing, and guerrilla gardening can be an empowering way to do this."

THE HOPE GARDEN

Lancaster West Estate, London

When news of the Grenfell Tower disaster reached footballer Tayshan Hayden-Smith, he returned home to Lancaster West Estate: the housing estate on which the tower stands. "It was a dark time," he reflects. "We were all living in a shared trauma."

Tayshan recalled how his late mother had turned to nature as an escape from the clutches of her illness: "She helped me see nature as a healing space, a freeing space."

Without knowing where it would lead, he began clearing a wide, gated patch of soil in the centre of the estate, and started to garden. "People would pass by and we would share a smile, or they would ask some questions. Each day, maybe two or three people would come by and say that they wanted to get involved."

"Slowly, slowly it grew. Every Sunday we'd go out; we'd play music, chat. People were more willing to talk in the garden. We'd lost so many people – family, close friends – there was obviously a real anger and sadness amongst us. The gardening lifted that."

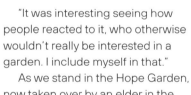

"It was interesting seeing how people reacted to it, who otherwise wouldn't really be interested in a garden. I include myself in that."

As we stand in the Hope Garden, now taken over by an elder in the community, Tayshan considers all he's achieved since this journey began. He now runs Grow2Know, a social enterprise bringing nature to the places and people that need it most. "It's all based around 'placemaking', where communities shape their own shared spaces." He's also writing a gardening book, and is a Director of Maxilla City, a grassroots co-operative reclaiming a huge deserted building in the estate as a multi-purpose community space.

When I boggle at how busy he is, he just smiles and says, "This isn't a job, this is my kids' future, and their kids' future."

"NONE OF US HAD ANY EXPERIENCE OF GARDENING, IT WAS JUST SOMETHING WE INSTINCTIVELY DECIDED COULD HEAL US. AND IT DID."

Tayshan Hayden-Smith

PROTEST

In refusing to comply with a status quo that says citizens must passively accept the state of their neighbourhood (however bleak), and that beautiful, biodiverse urban nature is a rarity, guerrilla gardening always carries an undercurrent of resistance. But it can also be wielded as a more intentional form of protest.

Perhaps the most (in)famous incident of guerrilla gardening as protest took place on May Day in the year 2000, when anti-capitalist group Reclaim the Streets gathered thousands of protestors in London's Parliament Square, armed with compost, trowels, and plants. The collective – who believed in community ownership of public spaces and opposed the centring of cars in urban planning – dug up the grass covering the square's central reservation and laid it across the road. In its place, protestors planted a variety of shrubs, herbs, and trees, created ponds, and even built a compost toilet.

Reclaim the Streets' May Day Protest, Parliament Square, London (2000).

Reclaim the Streets (then known as the group who'd bored holes into a motorway and planted trees in them) released a statement:

"Under the shadow of an irrelevant government, we were planting the seeds of a society where ordinary people are in control of their resources, their food and their decision-making... a world that encourages cooperation and sharing".

Though I support the message, the method was madness. Rather than showing how plants can make the world a better place, their purely temporary gesture (the plants were, to no one's surprise, immediately ripped out and laid to waste) had a net negative impact, costing time, money, and carbon to correct. Not only that, the scene on the day descended from peaceful celebration into violent chaos. Even anarchist Chris Wilbert, a sympathiser to the cause, called it a "mess".

If you plan on using plants as protest, take a leaf out of someone else's book. Like the Pothole Gardener, who highlights civic neglect of public roads and pavements (rather than drilling holes into them himself). Or Paul Harfleet (pages 114–115), who uses pansies to call attention to homophobia. You could plant climbers at the base of a billboard to quietly cover advertising, or write in moss graffiti to make your own statement – turn the page to learn how...

Paul Harfleet's piece "Was willst du? Komm doch! Ich hau dir eins in die Fresse!" ["Come on, I'll punch you in the face!"], planted and photographed as part of his ongoing Pansy Project.

PAINT THE TOWN GREEN

MAKE MOSS GRAFFITI

Moss graffiti is a (literally) green alternative to the chemical spray paints typically used to create street art.

GET EQUIPPED

Sheet(s) of moss

Kitchen spatula

Plastic/compostable carrier bag

Water spray bottle

Container with lid

Scissors

To make the paste:

1 cup buttermilk (or vegan yoghurt)

1 cup beer (or water)

1 cup flour

½ tbsp corn syrup (or golden syrup)

Small saucepan

Wooden spoon

01.

Find a sheet of moss growing outside on a shaded, damp urban surface in your neighbourhood, and gently remove it by sliding a kitchen spatula under it. Collect enough to cut your design from, but don't take too much from one place (only ⅛ of one particular sheet, at the most).

02.

Keep your moss sheet in a plastic or compostable carrier bag, and spray water to keep it damp. (The moss needs to be kept constantly damp throughout this process.)

03.

At home, combine the buttermilk (or vegan alternative), beer, flour, and syrup in a small saucepan, and gently warm over a low heat. Stir constantly, until it forms a gluey paste.

04.

Once it's reached a paste-like consistency, turn off the heat and allow your mixture to cool, then put it into a container with a lid on.

05.

As you wait for the paste to cool, place your moss onto a clean surface, and cut it into your chosen design, symbol, or lettering.

06.

Take your moss (once again in a dampened carrier bag) and paste to your chosen site. This should be a shaded wall, out of direct sunlight. Once there, remove your moss from its bag and cover the root-side (the brown side) with the paste, using your wooden spoon, a paintbrush, or your fingers (if you don't mind getting messy!) You don't need too much here: a thin but visible layer should be plenty.

07.

Once you've decided where you want your piece to go, gently press the paste-covered root side of the moss onto the wall, and hold in place for about a minute, until it's stuck.

08.

Spray your design with water before you go, and return frequently (daily, if you can) to keep it damp.

Another common method is to blend moss with the paste ingredients listed here (minus the flour) to create a spore-laden "paint". But this has a lower success rate than the cut-and-paste technique, and takes several weeks to grow in.

FIND A PLACE

ROAD VERGES, MEDIAN STRIPS,
TREE BEDS, PAVEMENT EDGES,
VACANT LOTS, ABANDONED
PUBLIC PLANTERS, BACK ALLEYS,
BROWNFIELD LAND...

This lifeless line-up may sound bleak but, to a guerrilla gardener, these places are full of excitement and opportunity. Soon, you'll see the world through these green-tinted glasses too. Here's what to look for...

SOILED FOR CHOICE

Forgive me for stating the obvious, but your chosen spot will either (A) have soil, or (B) it won't. This is an early choice to make when choosing a site for guerrilla gardening: are you looking for bare soil, or a bare hard surface?

SOIL

Finding threadbare or empty soil is the easiest way to start guerrilla gardening, and you may be surprised how much of it's around. Just take a walk around your neighbourhood with your eyes to the ground and you'll

soon discover plenty of patches that are notably lacking life. (Once you start looking, it's a blessing and a curse! Your eyes will be forever open to the ubiquity of barren streetside soil.)

Pages 58–69 provide examples of soil sites, featuring abandoned public planters, street tree beds, lawn edges, road verges, and vertical gardens.

NO SOIL

You can also decide to build onto paving, tarmac, concrete, or another hard surface. This opens up many more potential locations (most urban land is paved over), but necessitates an added step: either adding planters, or depaving.

Pages 68–77 provide examples of hard-surfaced sites, featuring vertical gardens, planters, depaving, vacant lots, and parklets.

MAP TIME

Tool Tip Use the map app on your phone to tag
potential sites as you pass them. My sense of
direction is terrible, so it's been a useful
way to re-find places I've whizzed past on a
bus. It also means you can identify potential
clusters of sites to tackle in a single day
and plan accordingly.

NEAR & NEGLECTED

There are lots of places you *could* plant, but where *should* you plant? A place should be two things to qualify for some ad hoc gardening: near and neglected.

NEAR

Guerrilla gardeners are on a mission, but we're not missionaries! We live *la vida local*: leaving our green fingerprints all over our own neighbourhoods – not others'. Choosing a spot near home also makes it much easier to plan, plant (especially when transporting heavy soil and water), and protect your site, as well as drum up local love and support for your grey-to-green wand waving.

NEGLECTED

There's not much added value in beautifying a beauty spot, sowing wildflowers in a wildflower meadow, or planting trees in a woodland – especially when there's more pressing work to be done elsewhere. Guerrilla greening gives us the power to inject nature where it's most needed: urbanised, derelict, and nature-deprived places.

Being local, you'll likely know a spot that's lain barren for years from a newly depaved area that the council are about to plant into. Opt for the former, armed with evidence of the "before" state, so if confronted by the local authority ("We're tending that space"), you're ready with the facts ("No you're not").

Leave wild spaces wild. Remember, we're working *with* nature, not disrupting it.

GREEN YOUR TURF

ALL DRESSED UP WITH NOWHERE TO GROW? LOOK FOR THESE...

The following pages contain examples of common sites you'll find to grow on. As with everything in this book, it's impossible to provide a comprehensive guide (the list of potential places is endless!), but these are useful and common launchpads for green takeoff.

CALIFORNIA GREENIN'

True Story The only time I've gotten in trouble guerrilla gardening was in LA - a non-local, with no one local guiding my action. The security guard's warning felt like poetic justice for abandoning the "act local" principle I bang on about.

ABANDONED PUBLIC PLANTERS

Well-intentioned councils like to scatter public planters around, only to run out of steam for maintaining them. These forsaken spots, having been designed specifically to host plants, are perfect for guerrilla gardening. If you can find one of these near you, it's possibly the best place to start!

Benefits include the fact that they're generally already filled with good-quality soil that's protected from getting compacted (i.e. repeatedly trodden on), and that people tend to assume any planting in them is municipal (meaning they're less likely to challenge its existence).

Check that it's definitely been abandoned – you don't want to end up in a silent war against a local council gardener, as they try to get their plants in and you yours. If you're local and see it often, you should have a good idea of how long it's been left like that.

Public planters are left abandoned all over the world: these photos show reclaimed planters in London, New York, and Tokyo (clockwise from top left).

WHY ARE PLANTING AREAS OFTEN NEGLECTED?

It's usually due to one of two things: lack of funding, or confusion over who's responsible for the spot. This can be down to internal ambiguity ("I thought that was your department's job?") or an external one ("Isn't that the other council's land?"). The giant bed claimed by Somerford Grows (pages 88-89) had been abandoned because the council thought the estate's TRA were responsible for it, while the TRA thought the council was.

STREET TREE BEDS

Tree beds, also known as tree pits, are the gaps in the pavement (or occasionally large planters) in which street trees are planted. These are also a great place to start! You'll find them in most neighbourhoods, usually bare at the base.

This nakedness is an unnatural state of affairs: trees love company! Wild trees usually have a host of smaller plants growing beneath their canopy, and planting under street trees can help recreate this healthy ecosystem. However, planting the wrong companions, or using the wrong method, can damage trees.

Creating and caring for a garden in a tree bed will mean you're supporting the tree, not only by protecting the soil it lives in but by watering it as you water your garden.

PLANT IDEAS

» **Bulbs** E.g. wild daffodil (*Narcissus pseudonarcissus*), snake's head fritillary (*Fritillaria meleagris*), wild tulip (*Tulipa sylvestris*).
» **Herbaceous perennials** E.g. meadow cranesbill (*Geranium pratense*), wood anemone (*Anemone nemorosa*), common cowslip (*Primula veris*).
» **Annual wildflowers** E.g. cornflower (*Centaurea cyanus*), common poppy (*Papaver rhoeas*), corn marigold (*Glebionis segetum*).
» **Winter interest** E.g. primrose (*Primula vulgaris*), lamb's ear (*Stachys byzantina*).

WHAT TO PLANT
DO

» Include native, resilient plants. Look to see which species are thriving in your area, especially in other local tree beds.

» Plant a diverse range of species, including ground cover among taller stems.

» Choose shade-tolerant plants if the tree casts a big shadow. Spring bulbs found in woodlands, like bluebells (*Hyacinthoides non-scripta*) and wild garlic (*Allium ursinum*), work well below deciduous trees, taking advantage of the spring sunshine before the tree has leaves.

AVOID

» Plants with a high demand for water, like hollyhocks (*Alcea rosea*) or sunflowers (*Helianthus annuus*), unless you plan to water the bed frequently. They can compete with the tree – especially if it's a young one – potentially killing both the tree and your plants.

» Planting climbers, such as clematis (*Clematis* spp.) and honeysuckle (*Lonicera* spp.), which could engulf the tree.

HOW TO PLANT IT
DO

» Maintain a distance of around 10–15cm (4–6in) between the base of your plants and the base of the trunk to prevent the bark from moulding.

» Plant densely, to cover the soil and help pollinators find the garden.

» Create a low wooden border around the edge, which will both protect your planting from being trampled and stop it spilling out and obstructing the pavement.

» Feed and enrich the soil where you'll be planting (but AVOID raising the soil level).

AVOID

» Harming the tree's roots: use a trowel, not a shovel, and work carefully around them; never pile soil or mulch up over the root flare (the bit where the roots join the trunk), as this can cause decay or hide root problems.

» Planting if the tree is a very young sapling (less than four years old), as any plants could outcompete it for water and nutrients.

REWILDING THE CITY

Camden, London

Corporate careerist-turned-guerrilla gardener John Welsh has come to be revered for his tree bed gardens.

As a child, John Welsh loved helping out in his parents' garden and, after finishing his studies, his first job was in a plant nursery. "But then I got pulled into a corporate career for 30 years," he sighs.

That began to change in 2016, when John's mother moved in with him and his husband. "She was shocked by the level of litter and dog foul in the street and suggested we plant some of the leftover plants from her old garden into the shabby tree beds outside." Sure enough, the plants flourished, and the mess around them subsided. "It was a revelation: I could actually change something, rather than just sitting at home like a pompous old fart, whinging or shouting at the council."

By the following year, John had created biodiverse gardens in six tree beds along the street, using only plants from saved seeds, cuttings, or division.

"GARDENING, WHETHER GUERRILLA OR NOT, IS ABOUT RESILIENCE."

John Welsh

People up and down the street stopped to ask what he was up to, and strangers turned to friends. The next year was set to look better than ever. But just as the hotly anticipated rainbow of spring blooms was set to emerge, Camden Council's subcontractor sprayed the entire street with glyphosate. "Everything died," John announces matter-of-factly. But the residents rallied together: donating whatever plants they could to refill the pits and committing to protecting them. Now, there are 15 tree bed gardens along the street and a group of neighbours help look after them.

The transformative experience inspired John to return to professional gardening: "I'm back to where I wanted to be when I was 21, but lacked the confidence to do it." He started Rewilding the City, an initiative working with communities to turn lawns into meadows and streets into eco-corridors.

"Gardening, whether guerrilla or not, is about resilience," he says. This means both personal commitment and building relationships: "Your community is the biggest support for any guerrilla gardening project. Don't just talk *at* people; ask questions, and listen to their answers." Relationships with the council can help, too: "Our street is no longer sprayed with glyphosate." Thank goodness.

LAWN EDGES

Our cities are so filled with squares of flat grass that, along with all the cuboid buildings, it can sometimes feel like living in a video game with cheap graphics. Though it's difficult to disrupt the middle of these spaces without much planning and preparation (and a campaign for their protection), the edges are usually easier to get creative with.

This is partly due to cultural norms (we've acclimatised to seeing decorative "borders"), and partly due to the simple fact that hired trimmers can't – or can't be bothered to – catch plants placed right at the edge of the space, especially if there's a fence, wall, or hedge in the way of their machine.

Under hedges, plant shade-loving plants like ferns and woodland bulbs, and native perennials. By fences and walls, you could scatter pollinator-friendly wildflowers, or even try climbers (page 68).

MARY MEADOWING

In Victorian England, a children's story called *Mary's Meadow* sparked a movement of people planting under hedges and along footpaths. In the tale, the eponymous heroine herself reads a story about a character who rambles the country sowing seeds as they go. In a double display of life imitating art, the fictional Mary's decision to try this herself was then echoed by the readers of *Mary's Meadow*, who took up this form of guerrilla gardening, or as they called it, "Mary-meadowing".

ROAD VERGES

Road verges are the strips of grass (and usually nothing more) that sit at roadsides. It's a catch-all term that includes the areas between roads and pavements, as well as the edges of motorways, dual carriageways, and so on.

The UK has over 313,000 miles of road verges in rural areas alone – a size equal to half the area of the nation's remaining flower-rich grasslands and meadows. But these would-be havens are often nothing more than grass monocultures, doused in herbicides that kill off vital food sources for native insects which, in turn, means no food for larger creatures.

If you want to rewild motorway verges, you can fling perennial native seed bombs from a car window. But, if the site is sprayed with herbicide, your work will likely be in vain. As long as these chemicals are around, our work will be twice as hard, and half as impactful.

Not only in this case, anti-pesticide action is a vital part of guerrilla gardening! (Pages 167 and 174)

BE SAFE!

Don't guerrilla garden on a thin, precarious strip of land if giant metal machines are flying by at high speeds. If you do go for a highway verge, make sure you have a safe crossing, and make sure you can be clearly seen: either go in the day, or wear hi-vis gear (which offers a double layer of protection in making you look "official"). If acting on a street verge, still keep an eye out, and always stay on the pavement side of the verge.

THE GARDEN OF EDEN CRESCENT

Kirkstall, Leeds

Eden Crescent is not your typical suburban street: its residents have transformed its road verges into an orchard, allotment, and wildflower meadow.

When chronic illness struck Grace Hills, she found gardening lifted her. Soon, this magic had spilled out beyond her own garden wall and brought the entire street together.

"As I'd potter about my veg planters, the neighbourhood kids would gather around to ask what I was doing and if they could help. It was alien to them – most front gardens in the area are concreted over. At the time, I was becoming increasingly involved in climate activism, and aware of future food insecurity. I thought: they've inherited a crappy future, the least I can do is share this joy and some skills with them."

So, she took her gardening practice out into the street; "our common ground", as she says. With their parents' blessing, Grace and her cohort of young enthusiasts have planted no less than seven fruit trees,

> **"OUR 'VEG ON THE VERGE' HELPS WITH THE COST OF LIVING, PROVIDES A HEALTH BOOST FROM GETTING OUTSIDE, AND SUPPORTS WILDLIFE."**
> **Grace Hills**

three vegetable patches, and two wildflower micro-meadows in the road verges of the aptly named Eden Crescent.

Grace was always eager to have the community's support, but never asked for the council's. "They say you have to pay them £250 to plant in a road verge on your street, and even then, only bulbs! That's just not right." After ignoring this restriction, and planting the first fruit tree with fellow residents, the council sent Grace an order to remove it. "I was wondering if I'd have to chain myself to it! Thankfully, when lockdown happened, they forgot all about it." Part of the reason they may have "forgotten" is that Grace's exploits brought the street together and led to Eden Crescent placing third in a nationwide competition to find "Britain's Friendliest Street".

Eden is spreading across Kirkstall: Grace recently rewilded 40 local road verges in as many days, using thousands of seeds she'd saved from local wildflowers the previous year. She says it's all down to determination: "A lot of people won't try something unless they have exactly the right conditions, but I'm very much a trial and error sort of person – just go for it!"

VERTICAL GARDENS

We tend to think of gardens in terms of a horizontal plane but – in places filled with tall, walled buildings – there's plenty of opportunity to grow *vertically*. Counterintuitively, buildings can actually provide even *more* room for nature than undeveloped land. Here's the maths: if you take a perfectly square patch of land and construct a cubic building on top of it, you end up with five times the original surface area.

There are three main ways to grow a gravity-defying garden:

CLIMBERS

Climbing plants *want* to grow up, making them a great option for blanketing a wall or fence in foliage and flowers.

» Climbers with tendrils (thin "arms" that reach around until they find something to grab on to, then curl around it), or twisting leaves or stems (where these parts of the plant work in the same way as tendrils) will need some support to hold on to. This makes them perfect for chicken wire fences.

» Climbers with sticky pads (does what it says on the tin) like Boston ivy (*Parthenocissus tricuspidata*) attach to the wall's surface, so won't bore into it and harm the wall.

» Avoid plants with clinging stem roots, like English ivy (*Hedera helix*), as these can cause the structures to crumble.

GROW UP

CRACKS & CRAGS

Have you ever noticed a plant growing defiantly out of the side of a wall? While taking care to avoid structural damage, you can encourage this phenomenon by sowing directly into urban walls.

» Consider what the surface is made of (for instance, limestone is alkaline, so won't welcome acid-loving plants) and which way the wall is facing to get the best chance of success.

» Alpine and coastal species thrive in the strange, hostile-looking nooks and crannies of urban walls, which mimic the crags they originally adapted to.

» **Suggestions:** common stonecrop (*Sedum acre*), yellow corydalis (*Pseudofumaria lutea*), creeping Jenny (*Lysimachia nummularia*), common harebell (*Campanula rotundifolia*).

STACKED PLANTERS

You can create a vertical planter with a series of troughs, either fixed to a backboard, or directly onto the vertical surface (wall, fence, and so on). Turn the page for a foolproof DIY planter.

MAKE A VERTICAL PLANTER

A novel way to make a vertical guerrilla garden using a bookcase.

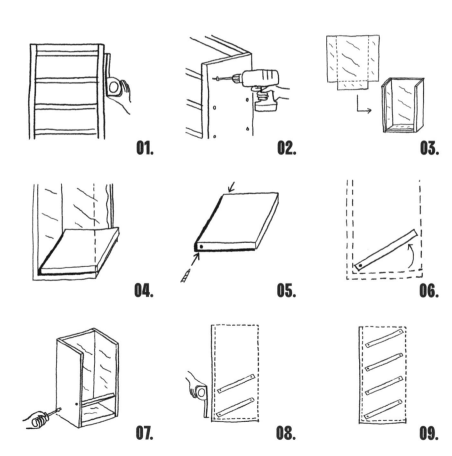

01.

02.

03.

04.

05.

06.

07.

08.

09.

GET EQUIPPED

Second-hand wooden bookcase

Tape measure

Screws

Drill or screwdriver

Plastic sheet (optional)

Staple gun (optional)

Compost

Plants

01.

Measure the distance between the shelves and make a note of this.

02.

Unscrew the shelves (by putting the drill in reverse) and remove them from the bookcase. These will become your troughs. (Depending on their state, you might be able to reuse the original screws!)

03.

Optional: Cut the plastic sheet to cover the inside of the bookcase and use a staple gun to secure it as a liner. This will help prevent the wood from getting damp and rotting over time. You could also cut and attach pieces of the sheet to the top of each shelf to line the inside of your troughs.

04.

Take a shelf and place it near the bottom of the bookcase, pulling it out about 1.5cm (about ½in) from the backboard. This gap between the shelf and the backboard will allow water to drain.

05.

Secure the back corner of the shelf's short sides by drilling them in place though the bookshelf's sides. Don't do this too tightly just yet, you want the shelf to pivot.

06.

Raise the front edge of the shelf (at roughly a 30° angle) to create the trough shape.

07.

Secure the top corner of the shelf's short sides tight by drilling them in place through the bookshelf's sides. Then tighten the screws you drilled loosely in place in Step 5.

08.

Taking the length you measured in Step 1, mark this distance above each of the four screws you've just put in place for the first trough. These are your screw placements for the second trough.

09.

Repeat this process for the remaining shelves until they are all secured as troughs.

10.

Fill the troughs with compost and plants.

If you can't find a bookcase, you can always make one of these from scratch by cutting panels of wood to size.

NO SOIL?
NO PROBLEM

The world's surface is increasingly paved. By one calculation, concrete already outweighs every tree, bush, and shrub on Earth. Does this leave us guerrilla growers with fewer and fewer options for planting? Nope. It only creates more need for it.

GEVELTUIN

The Dutch "geveltuin" movement is a type of depaving that involves flipping up paving stones outside your home to reveal the soil underneath, and then creating a "facade garden" in this newly-exposed groove. The movement began in the 1980s, when squatters in Amsterdam started to grow food in front of their squat using this technique. At first derided, the idea quickly caught on and is now actively encouraged by Dutch central and local government bodies. When I asked Jenny van Gestel, founder of GuerrillaGardeners.nl, about geveltuin as a mode of guerrilla gardening, she laughed and said: "It's so common here, it doesn't even feel like guerrilla gardening!"

There are two ways you can push against this blanket of grey: cover it in planters, or tear it up.

CREATING PLANTERS

There are many benefits to creating planters. For starters, you can put them anywhere, and even move them if you need to. You can also ensure that you fill them with healthy soil of whatever texture and acidity you need for your chosen living line-up. Though they can be used to cover ground, planters also free you from it: think about hanging baskets or hooked buckets.

If you're placing planters in the street, make sure they're not obstructing the path. If you're hanging them, make sure the fittings are strong enough to take the weight of soaking wet compost (so they're not going to fall on anyone's head!). And be wary of damaging existing street furniture (page 13).

DEPAVING

Depaving, as the name suggests, is the action of removing hard surfacing – paving slabs, concrete, tarmac, and so on – and restoring land to being an organic habitat. As well as providing a space to grow in, removing impervious surfacing reduces the urban heat island effect and allows for rainwater to drain (which helps mitigate flooding).

If you do decide to depave, firstly, right on. Second, do it right: only pull up paving where it's not needed and pre-plan what you'll do with the debris. Geveltuin set a groovy example.

Photos of guerrilla planters in London, Cork, Belfast, and Ottawa (clockwise from left).

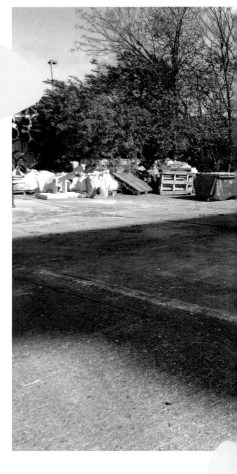

The vacant brownfield site in Hackney, London, that became the Garden of Earthly Delights' second incarnation (pages 96–97).

VACANT LOTS

As the literal foundation of the world, land is a source of freedom and power. How land is used, what's built (or grown) upon it, dictates where we can live, the air we breathe, what health services, education, economic opportunities, and leisure activities we have access to; whether we can be self-sufficient or condemned to wage dependency. It determines who can access the natural world, and who can exploit it. It shapes our quality of life, and even our way of life.

A finite resource, land should be used to maximise good for local ecology, community, and economic empowerment. Yet vacant urban land is a common sight. Understood in this way, reclaiming vacant land as a resource for public good is a reasonable and necessary act.

» About 17% of land in the USA's big cities lies vacant or abandoned, while around 10% of the nation's census tracts are identified as food deserts.

» In the UK, it's common for allotment waiting lists to be years long, while developers buy up plots of land as an investment, leaving them empty – and wasted as a social resource – for years.

Planting in "public places" can include making privatised land public again, as happens when guerrilla gardeners seize vacant lots and brownfield sites, turning them into permanent gardens, or using them as "meanwhile" sites. (*Sorry for the urban planning jargon! If you need them, you'll find definitions in the Glossary on pages 176–177.*)

PARKING LOT TO PARADISE

Navarinou Park is a community-run park in Exarchia, the neighbourhood known as Athens centre of radical political activism.

In 1990, the city's municipal council bought the space. They planned to turn it into a public square but, when urban development laws got in the way, the open space was leased as a car park for nearly 20 years. In 2009 (shortly after the lot had ceased to be used as a car park), locals seized the opportunity to create the community space that never was. They flooded into the lot, broke up the asphalt, laid in rich soil, and planted flowers and trees.

Today, the park includes a food-growing space and is still thriving under collective local management.

A FINITE RESOURCE, LAND SHOULD BE USED TO MAXIMISE GOOD FOR LOCAL ECOLOGY, COMMUNITY, AND ECONOMIC EMPOWERMENT.

PARKLETS

"Parklet" is both a diminutive of the word "park" (as they're tiny parks) and a play on the fact that they're placed into parking spaces. They generally involve some combination of seating and plant life and are based on the principle that more urban space should be given over to people and nature, and less to cars.

Though nowadays, parklets are not always guerrilla (as thankfully, councils are now putting resources into creating them), the idea sprung from guerrilla urbanism in the mid-00s.

PARK(ING) DAY

Park(ing) Day, held annually on the third Friday of September, is a global day of action in which guerrilla urbanists take over curbside parking spaces, repurposing them as pocket parks and places for social gathering.

The movement started in 2005, when artist, activist, and urbanist collective Rebar realised, for the price of a parking meter fee, "a parking space was an incredibly cheap piece of San Francisco real estate", and that there was no law saying these spaces could only be filled by a car. They laid down sheets of turf, wheeled in a tree, and set down a wooden bench in a parking spot in the Mission District, and soon had people around the world asking to recreate the piece.

They created an "Ikea-like how-to" which, along with a step-by-step process, shared principles such as:

"The fundamental elements of a good outdoor public space are seating, shade, a place to watch people and view scenery, and a sense of being in nature." From there, the day grew into an international phenomenon, birthing 15-square-metre gardens, music venues, game spaces, art installations, and more.

GATHER PEOPLE

MORE PEOPLE MEANS MORE KNOWLEDGE, MORE IDEAS, MORE SKILLS, AND MORE MANPOWER.

One of the beauties of guerrilla gardening is that you can always venture forth alone, with total anonymity and autonomy (I love a good solo adventure!), but it's undeniable that group operations make a bigger splash.

I recommend considering this step before you start planning a large project, so you can better meet local people's wants and needs, get advice from experts, and find comrades who want to see the garden survive and thrive.

There are three main ways people can get involved.

1. **IDEATION**
   Two heads are better than one.
   Bring together experts, locals, and other beneficiaries to co-design the garden.

2. **ACTION**
   Many hands make light work.
   Rope in some muscle to get the building and planting done.

3. **PROTECTION**
   There's strength in numbers.
   Stand together to withstand challenges and share upkeep responsibilities.

GUERRILLA GARDENERS ARE EVERYWHERE!

Your search for fellow rebels might be easier
than you expect. Often, when I tell someone
what I do, they'll share a story of their
own guerrilla planting quests.

True Story Once, as I was collecting scrap
timber from a building site on Haggerston
Basin, a friendly construction worker asked
what I was up to. After I explained the wood
was for guerrilla planters, he grinned and
pointed straight across the canal to a spot
where he'd helped his friend plant beside the
towpath with her (brilliantly named) guerrilla
gardening group, The Lost Plots.

RECRUITING

WHO TO FIND

LOCALS People who live around the site have a right to have a say in how it looks. They're also well positioned to keep the garden watered, clear of litter, and otherwise keep an eye on it.

SKILLS Help from people with horticultural expertise, community organising skills, and DIY workmanship is invaluable. You may find such resourceful people within the local community, or you could reach out to professionals.

Strong ecosystems are host to a diverse range of roles and functions. So, beyond the obvious skills, consider how the community's range of talents can help your project succeed. Are they artists, writers, coders? Filmmaker Tassia, for instance, created a film for Somerford Grows (pages 88–89), which helped them secure funding.

MUSCLE You'll need a task force to carry out the physical work. This is often the group who plan and protect the garden, but you may want to supplement these numbers with additional help on building and planting days.

AND HOW TO FIND THEM

You'll often start out in contact with a few other like-minded people, but how do you ensure your group is truly representative of the local community?

IRL OUTREACH
Ways to find people "in real life"

» **Leafleting:** Put the information up in local spaces (pages 84–85).
» **Door knocking:** Approach people in the neighbourhood directly (pages 86–87).

WHO ELSE?

```
ORGANISATIONS You might choose to partner with
a local community organisation or independent
business, either for financial support, or to
help give your garden immediate public "cred".
LOVED ONES You can also grab your mates! My
actions are usually half-filled with my nearest
and dearest. You'll still be introducing people
to the cause - various friends I've roped into
actions have gone on to create their own
guerrilla gardens.
```

» **Community Groups:** Look for local Tenants and Residents Associations (TRAs), youth centres, faith groups, cultural organisations, community kitchens, and volunteer groups.

» **Connections:** Ask your existing connections if they can introduce you to others.

URL OUTREACH
Ways to find people online

» **Social media:** Create a social presence, use hashtags related to your local area, and post in local groups (especially those related to gardening or community action).

» **Emailing:** If there's an expert whose help you'd like, reach out! You may be surprised how generous people can be with their time when it comes to meaningful projects.

» **Volunteer websites:** Look for volunteer organisations that operate near you.

Tool Tips

» **Nextdoor** is a site and app that hosts neighbourhood-specific feeds to create discussions and connections.

» **Meetup** is a social media platform for organising gatherings with people with shared interests.

» **GoodGym** is a UK-wide community of volunteers who get fit by doing good.

MIX IT UP

FOR ONE SPOT ON DALSTON LANE I...

Reached out to residents of the Peabody estate that faces onto the site by knocking on doors and leaving leaflets in letterboxes, and through residents I already knew.

Got invited to join the estate gardening group's WhatsApp, and added interested residents to the Dream Green one. On both, we discussed what they'd like the garden to contain, and who'd like to join in the action.

Listed an event on the Hackney GoodGym page, through which volunteers signed up to run heavy bags of topsoil to the site from local business Second Home (who had donated the soil), 15 minutes up the road.

Handed out leaflets to passers-by while working on the site, with a few joining Dream Green's WhatsApp group as a result.

LEAFLETING

Leaflets are a brilliant multi-purpose communication tool for guerrilla gardeners. You can post them through letterboxes, put them up in local spaces, and carry them with you on action days to explain to curious passers-by what you're up to.

DESIGNING

» **A picture speaks a thousand words.** Use them. They can highlight the problem, bring your green dream to life, and evoke a mood for your project.

» **Be succinct.** Limit text to the most important details. Lengthy pamphlets are more likely to go unread. Keeping to the core points allows people to fill in the gaps from their own perspective (and with their own motivations). It can also help strike up all-important conversations, as people may ask you to tell them more.

» **What to include:**

  » **The Problem**
  What problem are you addressing? Desolation? Fly-tipping? And why should the community care? Include a photo that highlights the issue.

  » **The Proposal**
  What's your plan to solve this problem, and how can they be a part of it? Create a visual representation of what the space could look like after.

PRINTING

» Call to Action
Treat the leaflet as an invitation with a clear call to action: join the group, follow us, or come to our next action day.

» How to Join In
Add your social handles, a QR code to join your WhatsApp group, or your personal contact details.

» Tool Tip
Canva can cover all your basic graphic design needs. It's a straightforward, free online tool, with loads of useful templates to take the stress out of creating a professional-looking design.

Find a way to do it for free, sustainably, or (ideally) both. You could ask a friend who works in an office to print them for you onto recycled or scrap paper, or contact an ethical, eco-friendly print company to ask if they'd support the cause.

SHARING

Put them up around your neighbourhood, in newsagents, bus stops, gyms, community notice boards, laundromats... Don't just put them up in the trendy local cafe, try to reach a diverse, realistic representation of the local community.

DOOR KNOCKING

Door knocking can be a great way to recruit neighbours to your cause, get feedback, and consider fresh perspectives.

It's not as scary as it sounds! Most people are lovely, and it can open the door (sorry) to brilliant conversations and connections you'd never have otherwise had.

WHEN TO GO

» Avoid times when people will be busy or tired.

» Weekday mornings are out of the question. Bed-headed, bleary-eyed, bread burning in the toaster... this is not the time to ask them about the tree bed up the road.

» After work? Better, but not ideal. Disturbing someone who's just got in from a long day, or is trying to eat their dinner in peace, isn't the best way to gain allies. Nor is it easy to inspire botanical insurrection as people are winding down for bed.

» My advice: go on Sundays, from 10am 'til 4pm.

» On Sundays – the day of wholesome leisure – people are more relaxed, friendly, and altruistic, as well as more likely to be home.

DON'T GO IF...

» You're ill.

» It's dark out.

» The weather is awful.

» You're in a bad mood.

they might want to get out of the project. This could simply be living on a nicer, brighter street, or they may want to connect to others and learn new skills.

» If they are interested, take down their details. If not, be understanding. Either way, offer them a leaflet (so they can follow along or reach out at a later date) and provide a clear idea of what will happen next.

HOW TO PREPARE

» **OUTFIT** Clothing is a non-verbal language. Neat and presentable says "trustworthy and competent", paint-splattered overalls say "fun and creative". What do you want to say?

» **KIT** Borrow a clipboard to take down the contact details of anyone interested and to clip your leaflets to. (As a free bonus: clipboards ooze credibility!) You'll need a pen too.

» **PITCH** Prepare and practise a sentence or two that explains your project in a clear, concise way. Ask a friend if it makes sense and sounds exciting.

» **BUDDY UP** Make sure you have someone to join you.

This makes it more fun, less daunting, and they'll be there in the unlikely event anything strange happens.

AT THE DOOR

» Respect people's homes from the moment you step into the surrounding space.

» Knock in a friendly way (yep, that really is a thing).

» Greet them with a smile and say your opening line explaining your project.

» As a mutual safety precaution, don't go into people's houses – stay on the doorstep while you chat.

» Answer their questions, and listen to their perspectives. Be patient and don't talk over them. Get an idea of what

IF SOMEONE ISN'T IN...

» Make a note of it and try to return later.

» Or, leave a leaflet in their letterbox, halfway in. That way, they'll definitely see (and hold) the information, rather than sweeping it straight into the bin.

AFTER

» Follow up with everyone who gave their details. Thank them, welcome them to the group, and reiterate what's happening next.

Remember, life gets in the way – many enthusiastic faces won't be present at the first action you organise, but keep them involved until they can join in.

SOMERFORD GROWS

Hackney, London

"The more people you involve, the bigger and better your project can become!" say these guerrilla gardeners.

Somerford Grove Estate was built in the 1940s with community and shared green spaces at its heart. Sadly, it had long suffered the effects of deep council funding cuts, leaving its lawns and beds bedraggled. Deciding to take matters into their own hands, Robin, Sulekha, and Tassia started Somerford Grows, a resident-led initiative to transform the neglected grounds. "We bonded over a shared desire to improve the estate, bring the community together, and foster a sense of belonging and ownership," Robin tells me. "The huge raised bed in the centre of the estate immediately struck us as the perfect place to begin."

Active listening and inclusion was a top priority. "We created a simple survey to ask other residents what they'd like to see happen with

the bed," they explain, "and brought it with us as we cleared the space of overgrowth and debris." Returning home from work or the school run and seeing the trio at work improving the shared space, people were naturally curious. "It was the perfect way to strike up informal, unintimidating conversations." Through those conversations, the group discovered that what the community wanted most was a herb garden, a colourful mosaic, and bright flowers to attract butterflies and bees.

But not everyone was happy about their plans... "There was hesitancy and distrust from some members of the Tenants and Residents Association". The group quickly got to the bottom of this: "There'd been previous projects where residents hadn't been properly consulted and had to undo unwanted changes, or fix things that had fallen into disrepair because the project was abandoned. Once we explained that the project was designed for and by us residents, and we were invested in keeping it going, they were incredibly supportive! They donated money, gave us a storage space, and put our information up on their noticeboards."

LOVE LOCAL PARTNERS

The group's impact grew with support from local community initiatives, including:

» A microgrant from Volunteer Centre Hackney's community support programme, Our Place.
» Advice on soil health and plant choices from social enterprise Hackney Herbal.
» A workshop for local children to co-design the mosaic from The Hackney Mosaic Project.

ACCIDENTAL ALLIES

Sometimes, you gain people's support without even having to try!

True Stories

» A patch of flowers I planted in a car park (and had shamefully neglected to water) had been thriving surprisingly well. I was flummoxed until I ran into a couple walking towards the patch with a water bottle. They'd recognised it as a guerrilla garden and had been watering it every time they walked past.

» I once returned to a site that I'd previously cleared of debris and started planting into, to find a stranger (I still don't know who it was) had put up laminated signs saying, "This is a garden, not a toilet", to protect it from... well, the obvious.

» During a visit to an abandoned planter I'd worked on, a woman rushed out of her house to proudly ask if I was looking at *her* guerrilla garden. Turns out, she'd made the most of the newly litter-free, enriched soil and had also been planting into it for months.

ROUGH SLEEPERS

Some sites that look perfect for guerrilla gardening may be home to rough sleepers. Given that guerrilla gardening is in the business of reclaiming public space for public good, in claiming a site as safe and comfortable accommodation, rough sleepers have a valid prior claim over our desire for flowers.

One of my earliest guerrilla gardening attempts was (for various reasons) doomed to failure. Besides the plot being too big for a first-timer, it turned out that the soft, sheltered soil was used by local rough sleepers. By planting into it, I was unwittingly creating anti-homeless architecture, while they were (understandably) ignoring my spurges and seedlings and staking their claim to the space they'd been using long before I decided to "rescue" it. So (despite pleas from other locals) I backed off and stopped interfering with the site.

REACH OUT

Beyond simply leaving rough sleepers alone, think about bringing them in - they're locals and neighbours too.

When the Garden of Earthly Delights realised two people were living on the "empty" site they planned to build on (though they never saw them), they left notes to them both, explaining their intentions and inviting the pair to a friendly discussion. They hoped to craft a plan for the site that worked for everyone, together. (Unfortunately, before the team received a response, the council, without asking, cleared the people's belongings.)

ORGANISING

There's no "correct" way to structure, organise, or communicate within your group. These decisions will depend on the unique people that make up your guerrilla gaggle. Here are just a few things to think about, which will help you work out what processes are right for your one-of-a-kind motley squad.

GoodGym Hackney and Dream Green volunteers carrying donated topsoil to a guerrilla garden in the making.

WHAT'S THE STORY?

You may know your project's purpose, but is everyone on the same page? Some people may be imagining a slightly different end result. Others might have different ideas about how you'll get there. Without a shared vision, your intentions and actions will scatter, meaning more time and effort put in, to lesser effect. In the tug-of-war against the neglect and scarcity of urban land, your crew need to be pulling in the same direction.

At the outset, craft a clear narrative, with a beginning (the "before" state), middle (your action) and end (the "after" result). This could be a grand long-term vision, or something as straightforward as "Plant bulbs in every tree bed on Station Road!"

Bring everyone into this common goal by listening to their motivations and aims, and seeing how your project can help fulfil them. You can either do this in a series of one-to-one conversations, or (if there are loads of people involved) create a survey as a listening tool.

Tool Tip
Google Forms is a great piece of free survey software.

COMMUNICATION

You'll need to set up a hub where you can share ideas and plans. Depending on the aims and structure of your group, you may want to use this just to broadcast information out, or as a group chat.

Tool Tip
Check out Geneva, WhatsApp, Meetup, Slack, Telegram, Trello, and Wickr Me, to see what's best for you.

Dream Green communicates over plain old WhatsApp, as do other community organisations I'm part of (including Hackney Urban Growers and the London Parklets Campaign). As it's an app people generally have already, it's a straightforward way to get everyone in one place, and ensure notifications aren't missed. However, it has its drawbacks and limitations, such as the single-thread feed.

STRUCTURE

Though guerrilla gardening is often framed as "random acts of gardening", its most effective operations are carefully considered: you'll need clear roles and goals to get things done.

You may want a leader (this could be you!), or opt for a totally flat hierarchy (as a caution: this becomes less viable as group numbers increase). If you do have a small group of equal leaders, meet up before you take action to arrive at a mutual decision. For larger groups, you'll need someone to drive things along and ensure everyone else is informed of the plan of action.

Bear in mind, as with almost everything in life, it's good to have a rough strategy from the outset, but allow room for things to evolve organically as you work out what does (and doesn't) work.

This step of the process was the hardest for me. I don't consider myself a natural leader, but have come to realise I do enjoy aspects of it: bringing people together and creating space for them to find fulfilment through fun, purposeful action.

THINK ABOUT

» **Commitment.** What kind of commitment do you need from people?
» **Talents.** Who's best placed to lead in which area of activity?
» **Principles.** Do you want to write a manifesto, or set up community guidelines?
» **Representation & Access.** What adjustments or accommodations might help people to join in?
» **Power & Privilege.** Is everyone in the group being heard fairly?
» **(Fun)ctionality.** How do you strike the right balance between having fun and getting things done?

MEETING UP

FINDING A GOOD TIME

If you've created a large group, I recommend setting a regular meet-up time. This could be 10am–12pm on the first Sunday of every month; it could be 6pm–8pm every Wednesday – it totally depends on you. The idea is that those who can make it, make it. For the others, there's always next time! Just let everyone know the meeting place, and what to bring.

For smaller groups, you may want to find a time that works for everyone.

Tool Tip

Create a poll on Doodle to find out when everyone can meet.

HAVING A GOOD TIME

Camaraderie from grassroots action is a feeling like no other. Cultivate it by holding space for people to relax and open up. Mad About Cork's Alan Hurley has a tip: "Before we do anything, we meet for a nice cup of tea! It's a great way to ease ourselves in, and welcome anyone new who might feel nervous."

To get to know each other better, create opportunities for people to share the little things they love. Perhaps you take it in turns to be "DJ" of the boombox playlist, or who chooses which cheap and cheerful local eatery to head to as a post-action celebration.

CULTIVATING COMMITMENT

There are a few ways to keep volunteers motivated and coming back for more:

» **NEW SKILLS** Ensure everyone has the opportunity to learn new things, both by doing, and from each other.

» **RECOGNITION** Recognise people's contributions, from compliments and thanks while you're working, to handing out "badges" for the number of actions they've joined.

» **NEW CONNECTIONS** Are they meeting like-minded people? How can you foster connections beyond the gardening action? Could you throw a street party or "garden party" when the garden is completed, or decamp to the nearest cafe (or pub) after action?

» **PROGRESS** Show that their actions are making an impact. Have seeds they sowed attracted bees? Has fruit appeared on a plant they watered?

THE GARDEN OF EARTHLY DELIGHTS

Hackney, London

How a break-in became a breakthrough for Hackney's community.

The Garden of Earthly Delights, a verdant sanctuary in the hectic heart of Hackney, burst into being in 2019, when an Extinction Rebellion faction broke into a vacant site in the nature-deprived zone. "It involved cutting a lock," confesses Seng, one of the garden's founding members. Within just a few weeks, artists, growers, and makers from the surrounding area had transformed the scrappy space into a lush community garden, using salvaged materials, borrowed tools, and donated plants. The opening celebration was a riot of live music, communal feasts, and talks on topics from urban permaculture to squatting rights.

From there, the group steadily grew in size, ideas, and abilities. "We started without a lot of

skills!" Seng laughs. "We learned as we went – by doing, and from each other." The project seemed unstoppable and grew strong support from the community, with workshops and fresh produce offered to all, free of charge.

Then, in 2021, the dreaded eviction notice came. "We always knew the space was earmarked to become a station entrance," says Domi, who helps manage the garden and its many volunteers. But they didn't give up. "We set our sights on an even bigger disused space, just up the road."

Thankfully, the council allowed the group to claim this fly-tipped scrapland. "But it was more important for us to get the community's approval," Seng explains. "We held a community assembly; we were flyering, putting posters up. There's always some opposing voices to start, but when you meet in person, break bread, and bring people into what you are doing, they suddenly see what it's all about. It's usually about people wanting to be heard, and feel included."

The garden is now flourishing on this second site. For now. As we speak, Seng's drafting a proposal – a plea to the council to keep it

"AS WE DEVELOPED, SO DID THE GARDEN; AS THE GARDEN DEVELOPED, SO DID WE."

Seng Cheong

that way. "They've already tried to move us, but we need this *here*: there's no other green space in the immediate vicinity." If they are forced to move? "There's no end to wasted spaces in dense, polluted areas. We have the skills to build on them. So that's what we'll keep doing."

CRAFT A PLAN

CRACK OUT YOUR CRAYONS, PULL UP A PINBOARD, OR GRAB SOME GLUE AND SCISSORS – IT'S TIME TO PLAN YOUR GUERRILLA GARDEN.

You know what it will be used for, who it will be used by, and where it will live – now you're ready to design your rebel plant parade! This step is all about planning what your garden will have in it: from plants, to structures, to creative touches.

IF YOU GET STUCK

1. **Don't panic.** Remember, plants want to grow! You just need to matchmake the right plants to the right places.
2. **Be flexible.** The final result will probably look different to your original vision. Allow your ideas to evolve organically and, as Tayshan Hayden-Smith puts it, freestyle.
3. **Phone a friend.** If you're feeling overwhelmed or unsure, ask for help. There will be an expert in your community web who's happy to share their advice!

"YOU CAN'T KNOW EVERYTHING WHEN YOU'RE GETTING GOING. YOU LEARN AS YOU DO. EVEN THE BEST GARDENERS GET THINGS WRONG! IT'S ALL EXPERIMENTS, A FREESTYLE — LEARNING HAS TO BE A JOURNEY OF EVOLUTION, JUST LIKE A GARDEN."

Tayshan Hayden-Smith

WHAT'S ALREADY THERE?

THE GOOD

Look for signs of life in your spot and try to protect them! Check for boreholes in the soil before you cover it (some bees and other species nest underground) and ID any "weeds".

Once you've identified the "weeds" growing there, see what role they play in the ecosystem and how they change across the seasons before you pull anything up (they may flower beautifully later in the year). What's growing there already can also provide hints as to the soil type (if you search what that species likes to grow in), which will steer you towards the kind of plants to choose.

Tool Tip

LeafSnap is a free app that identifies plants from photos with 98% accuracy.

THE BAD

Being a neglected urban site, you'll likely find some unwanted junk lying around. Litter is almost a given, but I've also found needles, broken glass, metal wires, knives, and faeces.

Safety first Clear the site wearing thick protective gloves, and safely dispose of any waste.

THE "UGLY"

There may also be some "messy" organic material, such as fallen leaves, bark, twigs, moss, and lichen. This supports local wildlife and enriches the soil, so think twice before removing it – you could collect everything in one place to create a bug hotel!

CHOOSING PLANTS

There are hundreds of thousands of known plant species on Earth, which might make choosing plants feel daunting...

Luckily, once you know the conditions you're picking plants to suit (including seasonal weather, amount of sunlight, and soil type), as well as your aims for the garden, this list narrows significantly, making the decisions much simpler.

In the pages that follow, I'll share some plant examples for reference. Please bear in mind these won't work for every set of circumstances, regional ecosystem, or climate – always do your own research!

NATIVE & INVASIVE

Native Species are those that either evolved into origin within a particular region, or migrated there and naturalised without human interference. Native plants are beneficial to the ecosystems they are found in because they've formed symbiotic relationships within the biome over many thousands of years, and so offer the most suitable sustenance and habitats for local wildlife. These should be your first choice when choosing plants.

Non-native Species, on the other hand, have been introduced to a region by (direct or indirect) human intervention. Many are harmless – or even beneficial – and naturalise (i.e. integrate into the local ecosystem). However, some can be invasive...

Invasive Species are so-called because they have the capacity to crowd out other species in the area, spread disease, or otherwise imbalance local ecosystems – possibly driving other species to extinction as a result.

Species generally become invasive as a result of human meddling: either disrupting an ecosystem such that a certain species is then able to take over; or introducing non-native species to a new region. Most countries (or regions) have a list of invasive species which it is illegal to plant or propagate.

For example, the deceivingly beautiful Himalayan balsam (*Impatiens glandulifera*) is currently running rampant across Britain's lowlands – blocking waterways, eroding river banks, and smothering native plants at an alarming pace.

Find out what's native and invasive in your area (page 174).

RETHINKING THESE LABELS: AN ONGOING DEBATE

These terms are widely used for practical (and legal) reasons. However, the glorification of "native" - along with the use of "non-native" in conjunction with "invasive" - has been used in eco-fascist and anti-immigration contexts. Beyond the political reasons to reevaluate these terms, many scientists now argue that the dichotomy of "native" versus "non-native" is becoming an outdated concept, as thousands of species are inevitably migrating to new regions as a result of changing climates.

GETTING TO KNOW YOUR SITE

Plants' needs vary: some like it hot, others dig shade; some need fertile soil, others aren't fussy.

In nature, plant species evolve over many thousands of years to adapt to certain climatic conditions. The better your understanding of the conditions at your chosen site, the better you'll be able to work with them, and so avoid dead plants and disappointment in the long run.

HEAT

How cold does your area get in winter?

This dictates how "hardy" your chosen plants need to be. Colder areas need "hardy" plants, whereas warmer areas can accommodate "tender" ones. The Royal Horticultural Society (RHS) has a plant hardiness rating system (page 174), which categorises plants from level H1 (plants that need to be kept in a heated greenhouse) to H7 (very hardy plants).

To find out how hardy your chosen plants need to be, search the average minimum winter temperature where you live, and compare this to each RHS plant hardiness category's

temperature range and description. Then look for plants with a hardiness rating equal to or higher than that! Most parts of the UK require a minimum plant hardiness of H4 or H5, though some (warmer) areas will accommodate H3 plants, and some (colder) areas require H6 or H7. If you're planting native plants, they'll already be adapted to local temperatures – another good reason to do it!

You may come across the United States Department of Agriculture's (USDA) hardiness rating system. It's fine to use this, as long as you don't accidentally combine the USDA and RHS systems, as their numbers correlate to different temperature ranges (1 is the warmest RHS rating and the coldest USDA rating).

3 hardy plants: dogwood (*Cornus alba 'Sibirica'*), heather (*Calluna vulgaris*), Swiss chard (*Beta vulgaris subsp. cicla var. flavescens*).

WATER
How much water will your garden receive?
Some plants need a lot of water. Others are drought tolerant. If you plan to water your garden frequently, you'll have many more plants to choose from. If not, you may want to avoid plants that need regular, year-round watering, and search for "drought resistant" species.

Even in famously rain-drenched England, gardeners increasingly have to contend with droughts and long, hot summers as a result of global temperature rises.

3 drought-tolerant plants: lavender (*Lavandula* spp.), daffodil (*Narcissus* spp.), wood cranesbill (*Geranium sylvaticum*).

LIGHT

How much sun hits your patch?
With regards to how much daylight they need, plants are grouped into three categories:

1. Full Sun: 6+ hours of sunshine a day
2. Partial Shade: 3–6 hours of sunshine a day
3. Full Shade: <2 hours of sunshine a day

To work out how much light your site gets throughout the year, it helps to know its "aspect", the compass direction it faces (North, East, South, or West). In the Northern Hemisphere, south-facing gardens receive the most sun – and vice versa. Then, see what surrounding it casts a shadow: trees will create dappled shade, whereas walls and buildings can block direct sunlight entirely. If you can, visit your site at different times of day, throughout the seasons, to learn how much light it gets and where.

3 shade-loving plants: snowdrop (*Galanthus* spp.), hart's tongue fern (*Asplenium scolopendrium*), knotted cranesbill (*Geranium nodosum*).

SOIL TEXTURE

What minerals compose the soil?
Soil gets its texture from differently sized mineral particles:

» **Sand** has the largest particles of the three minerals. This creates gaps through which air and water can move freely through the soil, helping oxygen reach roots and allowing for water drainage – often a good thing, though it can become very dry.

» **Silt** particles are the middling size, and silty soil feels smooth or floury to the touch. It's more fertile than sandy soil, but still free draining (unlike clay).

» **Clay** has the smallest particles of the three minerals, so creates a dense soil that can become waterlogged. Clay soil takes longer to warm up (over the course of mornings, and in springtime) than sandy soil, and is more easily compacted.

3 sand-loving plants: butterfly bush (*Buddleja davidii*), nasturtium (*Tropaeolum* spp.), viper's bugloss (*Echium vulgare*).

3 clay-loving plants: common yarrow (*Achillea millefolium*), rose (*Rosa* spp.), common barberry (*Berberis vulgaris*).

SOIL pH

How acidic is the soil?

pH is the measure of your soil's acidity or alkalinity. Generally, plants like slightly acidic to neutral soil, but urban soil can skew alkaline due to building materials and processes: cement, mortar, and limestone are alkaline. You can make soil less alkaline (i.e. more acidic) by adding sulphur dust or pine needles, but this isn't a long-term solution – it's better to find plants that suit the existing soil type.

3 plants for most pH levels: pot marigold (*Calendula officinalis*), coneflower (*Echinacea purpurea*), garlic (*Allium sativum*).

WITH ALL THAT SAID...

Your chosen planting scheme will likely be a combination of:

» Yes, researching to find the "perfect" plants. But also...
» Taking what you can get! Keep costs low (and reduce your carbon footprint) by adopting unwanted and donated plants (page 130).

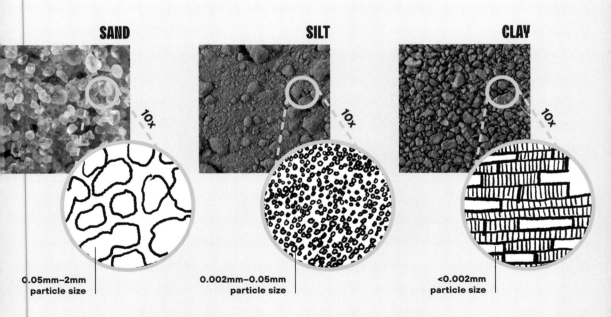

SAND

0.05mm–2mm particle size

SILT

0.002mm–0.05mm particle size

CLAY

<0.002mm particle size

10x

Loam soil contains all three particle types, allowing for air circulation, water retention, drainage, and fertility.

TEST SOIL

There are two key things gardeners test soil for: texture and pH level. *Guerrilla* gardeners should add one more test: toxicity.
For the most accurate results, carry out these tests before adding any organic matter to the soil.

ACIDITY

You can get basic pH testing kits from many garden centres and DIY stores for about a fiver (£5). Follow the instructions and match the resulting coloured solution to the pH chart (you might remember this bit from school): the yellow–red side of green means it's acidic; dark green, blue, or purple means it's alkaline.

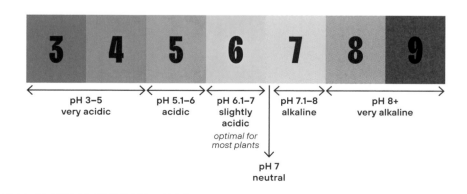

| 3 | 4 | 5 | 6 | 7 | 8 | 9 |

pH 3–5
very acidic

pH 5.1–6
acidic

pH 6.1–7
slightly
acidic
*optimal for
most plants*

pH 7.1–8
alkaline

pH 8+
very alkaline

pH 7
neutral

TOXICITY

Urban soil often has a complex history, so may contain toxins. Similarly to pH testing, you can buy a mail-order kit to test for heavy metals (e.g. arsenic, lead), hydrocarbons (e.g. petrol, diesel), and other contaminants (e.g. asbestos, pesticides).

Safety first If you want to grow food, the soil must be uncontaminated: the last thing you want is to poison anyone – well, I assume so! Instead of planting food directly into city soil of uncertain purity, fill planters with soil you know to be safe and healthy.

TEXTURE

GET EQUIPPED

» Trowel
» Cup measure
» Baking tray (optional)
» Metal sieve
» Water
» Ruler

GET READY

» Using your trowel, dig up 1 cup of soil from 10cm (4in) below the soil surface.

» Break up any lumps into small pieces, remove any sticks and stones, and dry the sample (you can spread it on a baking tray and put it in a warm oven to speed this up).

» Sieve the sample to remove any tiny stones, chippings, roots, or other matter (the soil particles are small enough to pass through the sieve).

» Gradually add water to the sieved soil until you have a playdough-like consistency.

Turn over to get going »

SIMPLE TEXTURE TEST

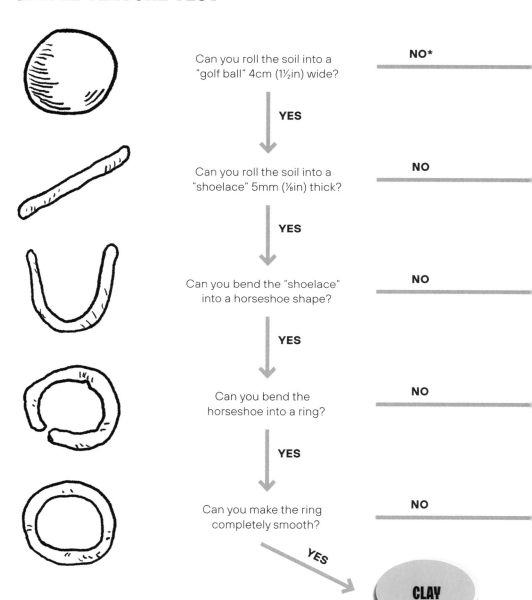

Can you roll the soil into a "golf ball" 4cm (1½in) wide?

NO*

YES

Can you roll the soil into a "shoelace" 5mm (⅛in) thick?

NO

YES

Can you bend the "shoelace" into a horseshoe shape?

NO

YES

Can you bend the horseshoe into a ring?

NO

YES

Can you make the ring completely smooth?

NO

YES

CLAY

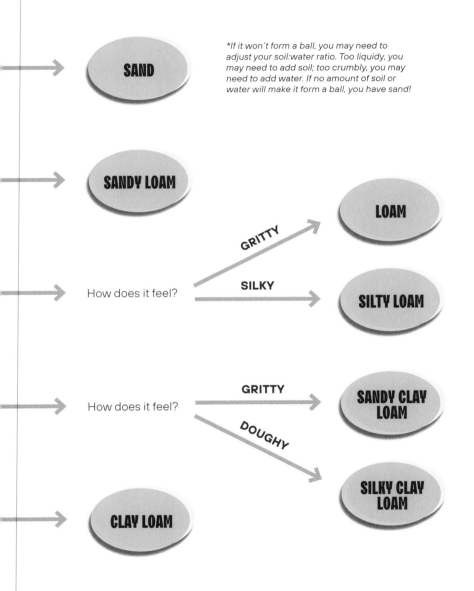

SAND

If it won't form a ball, you may need to adjust your soil:water ratio. Too liquidy, you may need to add soil; too crumbly, you may need to add water. If no amount of soil or water will make it form a ball, you have sand!

SANDY LOAM

LOAM

GRITTY

How does it feel?

SILKY

SILTY LOAM

GRITTY

How does it feel?

SANDY CLAY LOAM

DOUGHY

SILKY CLAY LOAM

CLAY LOAM

If you can't (or would prefer not to) touch the soil, you can also order a testing kit to determine the soil's texture.

TYPES OF PLANT

ANNUALS Annuals germinate, produce leaves, stems, and flowers, set seed, and die – all within a single year.

BIENNIALS Biennials are similar to annuals, but have a two-year life cycle: in year one, they germinate and grow; in their second year, they flower and set seed.

Some annuals and biennials "self-seed" (or "self-sow"), meaning they drop seeds to the ground before they die. This means you'll see the same (looking) plant grow back again! It will be their offspring growing from seed, however, not the same plant regrowing from the root (as with perennials).

PERENNIALS Perennial plants have long-lasting roots that survive through the seasons, allowing the plant to grow back, year after year. Herbaceous perennials die down to the ground in autumn and regrow in spring; evergreen perennials keep their leaves all year round.

Although shrubs and trees are technically perennials, you will mainly hear the word "perennial" used to refer to non-woody flowers and foliage.

BULBS In gardening, the word "bulb" is commonly used to refer to various kinds of bulbous underground food-storage system, including true bulbs, corms, tubers, tuberous roots, and rhizomes.

SHRUBS Bush-like plants with woody stems that, like trees, can either be evergreen (meaning they don't shed their leaves in winter) or deciduous (meaning they do).

INTERNATIONAL SUNFLOWER GUERRILLA GARDENING DAY

On May 1st (May Day) every year, guerrilla gardeners throughout the Northern Hemisphere sow summer splashes of yellow in public places across their postcodes. The global event began in Brussels in 2007, and since then thousands of guerrilla gardeners have participated. Sunflowers (*Helianthus* spp.) are big, beautiful, resilient plants. They're also edible! Not only their seeds - you can find recipes for everything from their shoots to roots to petals. *If you plan on eating your sunflowers, check the soil is healthy first.*

TREES I know you know what trees are, but to complete the set... Trees are large, woody perennials that typically have a tall, thick stem (a "trunk"), from which lateral branches grow, which can produce leaves, flowers, and fruit.

POWER PLANTS

After searching for plants that directly fulfil your garden's purpose (e.g. "pollinator-friendly wildflowers", "pollution absorbing shrubs", or "easy-to-grow vegetables") consider adding plants with other benefits:

DYNAMIC ACCUMULATORS

These plants' deep roots bring nutrients up from the lower layers of soil into their leaves. When they die and their leaves fall, the nutrients flow into the soil's top layer, benefitting other (more shallow-rooted) plants.
3 examples: chickweed (*Stellaria media*), borage (*Borago officinalis*), dandelion (*Taraxacum officinale*).

NITROGEN FIXERS

Plants need three key nutrients: nitrogen (N) for leaf growth; phosphorus (P) for root and shoot growth; and potassium (K) for flower and fruit growth, and overall hardiness. Legumes have nodules on their roots that convert nitrogen from the air into a form that plants can absorb from the soil.
3 examples: common vetch (*Vicia sativa*), red clover (*Trifolium pratense*), sweet pea (*Lathyrus odoratus*).

COMPACTION CRACKERS

Compaction is a common problem for streetside soil in public places. Some plants, like legumes, can break apart compacted soil. Plant or sow these in a layer of organic matter on top of the compacted soil, and their roots will dart down and break it up.
3 examples: broad bean (*Vicia faba*), potato (*Solanum tuberosum*), spear thistle (*Cirsium vulgare*).

REMEDIATIVE PLANTS

Through "phytoremediation", these plants draw out hazardous contaminants such as heavy metals, pesticides, explosives, and crude oil. Make sure you dispose of them safely afterwards – don't eat them or add them to the compost pile.
3 examples: willow (*Salix* spp.), sunflower (*Helianthus* spp.), mustard greens (*Brassica juncea*).

HARDY, LOW MAINTENANCE, DROUGHT-TOLERANT PLANTS

Search these criteria to find plants that are pretty indestructible, and can survive with intermittent care, to make life easier for yourself while giving your garden the best chance of survival.
3 examples: firethorn (*Pyracantha* spp.), lesser periwinkle (*Vinca minor*), cornflower (*Centaurea cyanus*).

THE PANSY PROJECT

Global

The artist and "accidental activist" using guerrilla gardening to call attention to homophobic and transphobic hate crimes.

Paul Harfleet's process is simple: he finds the nearest patch of soil to the incident and plants a single pansy (*Viola tricolor*). Since 2005, he's planted over 300 "gestures of quiet resistance" around the world.

The Pansy Project, as it's now known, started with "a string of homophobic abuse on a warm summer's day," Paul recalls. "Threats, stone-throwing, insults. I was thinking about how I'd have to walk past those places every day, and wanted to change how I felt about them. I thought about roadside memorials, floral memorials, and how they change the way you experience a space. I wanted to use that language to talk about hate crimes."

Since then, Paul's peaceful, planted protests have paid respect at scenes of verbal abuse, physical attacks, and murders. Homophobia has dug these living monuments into the ground beside the Stonewall Inn,

"I TRY TO MAKE THE PANSY LOOK AS STRONG, POWERFUL, AND RESILIENT IN THE IMAGE AS POSSIBLE."

Paul Harfleet

*"Misbegotten Pansies",
Brooklyn Bridge, New York
(right). "Beaten!" Kungsgatan,
Stockholm (left).*

outside the United Nations headquarters, and in the shadow of the White House. "Like other guerrilla gardening, it's about the politics of public space, and how and where we demonstrate," says Paul. "It appears to be silly, but it's actually very dark."

Does the project show any signs of slowing? "When I started I thought, naively, that it would gradually fade into social tolerance and acceptance. But the pendulum swings from one issue to another – transphobia has really risen up – so the project has evolved."

Paul is happy for others to follow in his footsteps, but does share words of warning. "If you're marking your own experience, that can be cathartic. But it takes its toll, going into this world of hate." He also cautions that you can be vulnerable: "Once, someone spit 'fucking f****t' at me as I was planting. It was surreal, I then had to put a second pansy in the same place."

WHY PANSIES?

The name holds a double meaning: "pansy" is a homophobic slur ("I've been called a 'pansy' before", Paul recounts); but the bowing-headed flower's name originates from the French *pensée*, meaning "thought". What could be more fitting as a statement for solemn reflection on homophobia?

PLANTING SCHEME

Invest some time in planning the layout of your planting before you start putting things in the ground. This is not only important for aesthetic reasons, but impacts the plants' health too.

There aren't really any "rules" when it comes to choosing how to arrange your plants, but two principles are always good to keep in mind:

DENSITY

Urban streets can be harsh environments but, when grouped together, plants can help look after each other and form micro-ecosystems that help other life too. When planting for density, think about:

1. **CLUSTERS** Planting or sowing clusters of the same plant type will help pollinators and other local wildlife to find the garden, as well as giving it visual impact.
2. **GROUND COVER** Bare soil is a wound in the Earth. Use low-growing, spreading plants to cover gaps, and so keep the soil underneath healthy.
3. **GROWTH SIZE** When mature, the plants should just be touching each other. If you're starting with young plants that will get bigger, leave some space around them to grow into.

"I SPENT A LOT OF TIME FIXING MY FIRST GARDEN. THINGS WERE TOO CROWDED (I'M FROM BRAZIL, SO I DIDN'T KNOW HOW BIG NYC-NATIVE PLANTS WOULD GET!); THERE WERE SMALL PLANTS IN THE BACK AND TALL PLANTS IN THE FRONT. THE SECOND TIME, I ASKED A LANDSCAPE DESIGNER TO HELP ME PLAN IT RIGHT FROM THE START."

Simone Marques

DIVERSITY

Don't be a one-trick peony – whatever you choose to plant, choose more than one species. Here's why:

1. **IMPACT** Different insects, animals, and people want different things from plants. Planting a range of species means there's more likely to be something for everyone.
2. **BEAUTY** Choose plants with different heights and sizes to keep things interesting on the eye, and aim for year-round interest with plants that flower at different times of year and perennials with interesting autumn foliage or architectural stems and seedheads.
3. **RESILIENCE** "Companion plants" support each other's needs: boosting nutrients, distracting or repelling predators, attracting beneficial insects, providing needed shade, and so on.

BUG HOTEL Bug hotels vary in size and complexity, but essentially create bedding for native insects, often using a combination of sticks, old wood, pine cones, hollow bamboo, and straw.

COMPOST BIN Creating a community compost pile means an endless source of organic fertiliser for your garden.
Tool Tip: Visit MakeSoil.org or ShareWaste.com

EDGES Border your planting with well-secured wooden boards, a row of bricks, logs, or large stones. This will signal to people (and dogs, who are spatially aware of borders) not to use your garden as a pavement (or toilet).

FENCES You may want to construct a fence around your garden. Keep accessibility and inclusivity in mind – if your garden is for everyone to enjoy, don't bar them from entry.

BEYOND PLANTS

Beyond plant choices, your plan should take into account how your garden can be more inclusive, impactful, and fun!

FUNCTIONAL STRUCTURES
What structures could help your garden fulfil its purpose?

BOOK EXCHANGE A glass-fronted box, filled with free books. You could create a themed collection, or invite anyone to leave donations for others.
Tool Tip: Visit LittleFreeLibrary.org

LOCKS Bike locks can be used to secure planters and furniture in place, to hold them fast and stop them getting nicked.

PATHS Paths invite people into the garden, while keeping them off the plants. Look for existing "desire paths" (paths created by people repeatedly walking across or through a space) on the ground and avoid planting on these, or accentuate them with borders, or by laying down woodchip, stone slabs, or gravel.

PLANTERS Plant pots or raised beds are essential for paved sites (or sites where the soil is contaminated), and mean you can control the type of soil you grow in.

SEATING Seating invites people to spend time in the garden. You can arrange seating to encourage conversation, or see a lovely view.

SWING You could (securely) fit a hanging swing or other play structure for the young and young-at-heart to have fun with.

MEASURE THRICE, CHECK TWICE, CUT ONCE

If you're making furniture or other features from scratch, remember to double (and triple) check your measurements – both of the garden space and your materials – before building.

TABLES Tables invite people to do more than just sit in the garden – they make it easier to eat a picnic, play a game, or have a cup of tea.

WATER COLLECTION Could you create a water-saving system to direct rainwater to your garden, or save it in a tank for future use?

CREATIVE TOUCHES

How can artistic flair inject more joy and fun into your garden?

CHALK ART Draw ephemeral art on the pavement with chalk.

"CLEAN GRAFFITI" Use a pressure washer to create "clean graffiti" on grubby paving by jet-washing through a stencil.

MOSAIC Add a meaningful mosaic to your space, à la Somerford Grows (pages 88–89).

MURAL Paint a huge mural yourselves, or get a street artist on board.

SCULPTURE Create an outdoor sculpture from weather-proof repurposed materials.

SIGNS Paint on wood planks to create signs that put a smile on someone's face.

AVOIDING ABLEISM

Around 1 in 5 people in the UK are disabled. To create a guerrilla garden that truly maximises public space for public good, ensure your garden (and the group activity that makes it) is accessible, safe, and welcoming – rather than an inconvenience – for people with motor or sensory impairments, and Neurodiverse people.

WHERE TO START?

» **STRUCTURAL BORDERS**
  Creating raised edges around your planting will:
  » Keep plants off the pavements, preventing obstructions for wheelchairs and mobility scooters, and avoiding trip hazards for the blind.
  » Help people who use canes to feel the edges of your garden.

» **CLEAR PATHS** If you create paths, ensure they're wheelchair-accessible in terms of width – at least 1m (3ft) – and materials. Keep existing paths free from obstruction too.

» **RAISED BEDS** Using planters that are around 0.75m (2.5ft) high will help wheelchair-using guerrilla gardeners reach the plants and soil.

» **SENSORY PLANTING** Avoid plants that are toxic or painful to touch, and include ones blind and Neurodiverse people (and others) can enjoy, such as:

  » **Scented Plants** E.g. lemon balm (*Melissa officinalis*), sweet woodruff (*Galium odoratum*), creeping thyme (*Thymus serpyllum*).
  » **Soft Plants** E.g. lamb's ear (*Stachys byzantina*), silver mound (*Artemisia schmidtiana* 'Silver Mound'), pussy willow (*Salix discolor*).

» **COMMUNICATION** As well as physical aspects of your project, ensure that your digital communications are accessible too: write image descriptions and alternative (alt) text for images; add closed captions to videos; ensure there's sufficient contrast between text and backgrounds; and use CamelCase (capitalizing every new word) in hashtags and account tags.

A GUERRILLA'S ADVICE

Corkonian painter and photographer Peter Mahony has guerrilla gardened with Mad About Cork (MAC) for years. He says:

EVERYONE HAS SOMETHING TO OFFER

"Being in a wheelchair means I can't always do the hard labour (though I've certainly done my share of moving things!) but I've planted and painted plenty, and have found my own space in the group with my camera - being able to record everything is very fulfilling."

HELP ALLEVIATE STATE ISSUES

"Most problems with accessibility are presented by the city itself, rather than the work we do. For instance, when moving to another location, I might not be able to take the shortest route because of the state of the footpaths. In those situations, someone would always be happy to accompany me."

LISTEN & LEARN

"Of course, I can only speak for myself here! I can't speak for people with other disabilities - so listen to what they have to say. If you want to be more actively inclusive, contact a dedicated organisation that works with disabled people, and host joint events."

MAD ABOUT CORK

Cork, Ireland

From a pair of artists to a community movement, local pride is breathing new life into Cork with paint and petals.

For decades, awash in a tide of recession and state neglect, Ireland's ancient city of Cork (Corcaigh) had been falling into dereliction. One day in 2015, as artist Alan Hurley wandered through his hometown, the streets felt bleak enough to call for immediate action, and bright enough to inspire it. Walking along a thin, dirty alleyway, he began picking up rubbish as he went. Head bowed, treading forward, Alan bumped into someone (literally) who happened to have had the same epiphany. "That was how I met Owen!" he tells me.

The pair immediately hit it off, and together their ambitions grew. Looking around them at fenced-off, forsaken concrete yards, blackened sites of burned-out buildings ("Insurance," Alan explains), and run-down roadways, the pair decided to use street art and guerrilla gardening as an antidote to dereliction.

They chose a first site that could only get better: Coleman's Lane.

"EVERY SPLASH OF PAINT AND PLANT IS A STATEMENT: WHY ARE DERELICT SPACES LEFT THIS WAY?"

Alan Hurley

Once a Viking laneway, now a hotspot for drug use and defecation. "The city wanted to close it," Alan says, "but without it, elderly people faced a long walk-around to get into town". They decided to flood the lane with colourful paint and petals. "We saw it as an experiment! We didn't know how to garden, I'd never painted a mural. We found ourselves standing over pallets like 'shit – how do you take these apart?'" Luckily, after putting word out, the group quickly grew, bringing in new skills, knowledge, and manpower. Soon, the lane was transformed. "When everything started blossoming we were like, 'Jesus!' We didn't expect the worst lane in the city to be this nice." As a result, the city kept Coleman's Lane open.

The group went on to transform dozens of dingy places across the city, including painting electrical boxes with global flags "to show that everyone's welcome here". A born and bred Corkonian, who has no plans to leave ("I think I'll be here all my life"), Alan is staking his right to improve his city. "Sometimes people will say, 'I want to do this, who do I ask?' Don't ask! Just go ahead. I'm proud of my city, and I'm proud of what we've done for it."

GET THE PARTS

WHAT TOOLS, MATERIALS, AND OTHER PROVISIONS DO YOU NEED TO CREATE YOUR GUERRILLA GARDEN, AND HOW WILL YOU GET THEM?

STAPLES

» **PLANTS** The real stars of the show, plants (or seeds) are the only truly essential item for guerrilla gardening.

» **GARDENING TOOLS** Depending on what you're planting, you may need a trowel, hand fork, bulb planter, spade, and/or garden fork. Spares are helpful – passers-by often ask to join in!

» **GLOVES** Protect your hands from sharps, solids, and toxins in dodgy urban soil.

» **COMPOST** Bags of (ideally homemade) peat-free compost to enrich the soil. *Why peat-free compost?* Peat comes from peat bogs. Mining peat from these ancient ecosystems releases CO_2 into the atmosphere and destroys rare, finite habitats.

» **WATER** Bring a vessel like a watering can, office water-cooler tank, jerrycan, or plastic bottle. Fill it up as close to the site as you can – water is heavy!

» **BIN BAGS** Bring black bags and recycling bags to collect litter from the street and any packaging you can't reuse. Bring garden waste bags for sticks, dead leaves, and any plants you pull out or cut back, or throw them on a compost pile.

EXTRAS

» **SNACKS** If you'll be going for a while, bring some fruit or biscuits to share around (check if anyone has allergies before whipping out the Snickers). Make sure there's water for people as well as the plants, especially when it's hot out.

» **SPEAKERS** Playing some tunes creates a fun atmosphere and helps people relax and enjoy themselves, making the work feel easier. It can also encourage others to join you.

» **DIY KIT** Are you adding any additional elements beyond plants? If so, remember to bring everything you'll need – paint, paintbrush, planks of wood, nails, hammer, and so on – to get it done.

» **FIRST AID KIT** You might want to bring the basics with you, in case of any scrapes.

» **LEAFLETS** If you'll be there a while, you're likely to get a few interested passers-by! Explain what you're about and how they can get in touch.

» **WHEELS** Carrying all your kit is so much easier if you use a wheelbarrow, pull-cart, suitcase, shopping trolley, or wheelie bin.

SUSTENANCE & SOUNDS MAY BE PROVIDED FOR YOU...

True Story People often bring tea, coffee, and biscuits out as a thank you. One particularly lucky day, a pub across the road brought us two crates of cold beer, while two-man band *The Cash Cows* stopped to serenade us.

THE SUBVERSIVE GARDENER

New York & London

Can't find the right tool for the job?
Why not invent your own?

A pair of suited young professionals walk along London's embankment beside a featureless soil verge. The man puts his briefcase down, reaches inside, then picks it up and walks away. The woman follows, swinging her handbag as she goes. Nothing to see here. Except there is: a geranium has appeared.

How? Concealed inside the briefcase is an auger, which bored into the streetside soil. The perennial dropped into this hole from a trapdoor in the handbag. Both tools were created by designer Vanessa Harden – along with loafers that plant a seed every 20 steps and a camera that shoots them longer distances – as part of a collection inspired by Ian Fleming's ingenious inventor, Q.

Vanessa, under the alias The Subversive Gardener, devised these cleverly covert contraptions in 2009.

It was a time when guerrilla gardening was blooming, but was very much a furtive, underground affair, often done under cover of night. More recently – in step with the cultural shift towards loud and proud guerrilla gardening – Vanessa

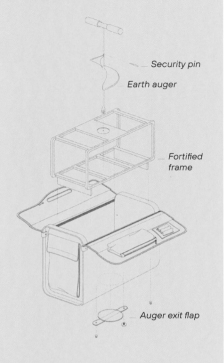

Security pin

Earth auger

Fortified frame

Auger exit flap

(Clockwise from above) "Tools by Q" handbag and briefcase; blueprint for the briefcase's boring mechanism; miniature trowel nail ring; seed shooter grills.

created attention-grabbing wearable tools, including grills that fire seeds from a telescopic pea-shooter, and a set of miniature trowel nail rings. These statement 24-carat gold-plated pieces were featured in British *Vogue*, bringing radical growing to an unlikely audience.

If you were hoping to get your hands on one of her spy-style inventions, sadly, they aren't for sale. "I'm not interested in making money from them," she explains, "my aim is to promote discussion and inspire people to create their own guerrilla gardening tools." Vanessa does more than provide inspiration, she actively helps people do this, hosting workshops and organising events that connect communities with designers and engineers. "I'm a big believer in tools in general," she says, "but especially DIY tools."

"I'M A BIG BELIEVER IN TOOLS IN GENERAL, BUT ESPECIALLY DIY TOOLS."
Vanessa Harden

GETTING THINGS CHEAPLY & CONSCIOUSLY

Getting the parts you need shouldn't cost the Earth – metaphorically or literally.

Sometimes, buying things cheap comes at the planet's expense. But there's also a huge overlap between getting things ethically and cheaply.

Before buying new, first see if you can borrow. If not, repurpose what you already have. Finally, see if you can buy second-hand. If you do buy new, buy to last (and lend it out, or sell it on when you no longer need it).

IRL SOURCES

» **Your group** may already have their own tools, or plants that could go in the garden.

» **Lending libraries** or "tool libraries" loan out gadgets, appliances, and tools (a handsaw is around £1.50/day).

» **Construction skips**, but first check that the item you want isn't needed. For health and safety reasons, builders aren't allowed to say, "Yes, you can take that!" But you'll likely hear, "I'll pretend I didn't hear that..." as they wink and turn away.

» **Recycling projects** in your area that rescue and redistribute items like scaffolding wood, fabric, furniture, and paint for local reuse.

» **Ask a local community garden** where they got plant or material donations from.

» **Pallets** are the guerrilla gardener's clay: they can be transformed into just about anything.

FOR PLANTS

» **Garden centres** may donate plant stock they can't sell (just check it isn't diseased).

» **Tree nurseries** often donate plants for community causes.

» **Propagate** plants from cuttings, or by division (pages 136–139).

» **Save seeds** from plants and food (pages 136–137).

URL SOURCES

» **Nextdoor.com** is an online neighbourhood noticeboard that makes it easy to find local growers, makers, and community-lovers, who are often happy to share or lend things.

» **Digital marketplaces** can unearth everything you need (and some things you didn't know you wanted). Try Freecycle, Geev, Craigslist, Facebook Marketplace, or Gumtree.

REUSING PALLET PLANKS

When repurposing industrial pallets, look for the lettering on the side:

OKAY TO USE:

✓ HT (Heat Treated)
✓ KD (Kiln Dried)
✓ DB (Debarked)

DO NOT USE:

✗ MB (Methyl Bromide)

This means chemically treated, and the chemicals may leak into your soil.

FUNDRAISING

» **Crowdsource** on a site like Spacehive or GoFundMe.
» **Sell** things or run an event – from the traditional bake sale route, to hosting a workshop or film screening.
» **Search for grants** or trusts to develop your area.
» **Ask local community organisations** for a microgrant (they can also provide feedback on the idea, connections, and other support).

TURN (ALMOST) ANYTHING INTO A PLANTER

What do an old football, colander, welly, dresser drawer, and milk carton have in common? They're all guerrilla planters waiting to happen.

GET EQUIPPED

A weatherproof object you can make holes in the bottom of

Screwdriver (or drill)

Scissors

Coir lining

Soil

Plants

Optional:

Strong natural rope

S-hooks

01.

Carefully poke holes in the bottom of your chosen object with a screwdriver to allow water to drain out (don't stab yourself).

02.

Cut the coir (coconut fibre) mat to size.

03.

Line the inner base of the object with the mat to stop the soil from falling through the holes.

04.

If you're going to hang your object – see "optional" steps (*right*).

05.

Fill your holey object with whatever soil is right for the plants you want to put in it.

06.

Pop your plants in *et voilà*! Your planter is now complete.

07.

Place it somewhere securely.

Optional:

To hang your planter up...

» Create 3 or 4 holes around the object's top edge.

» Cut the same number of pieces of rope/twine as you have holes – cut them all to the same length.

» Tie each piece through a hole and secure it tightly (now is a good time to learn some knots).

» Tie them together at the top, either all together or in pairs.

» Slide S-hooks through the knot(s) where the ropes join, or tie the rope directly onto the place you wish to hang it from.

» Once the planter is full of soil and plants, hang it securely from a load-bearing support. Check the rope is strong enough to take the weight of wet compost.

SEED STREETS BROOKLYN

Bushwick, Brooklyn, NYC

Artist Melynda Gierard creates sculptural guerrilla gardens using found objects: chairs, railway-crossing barriers, tyres, and more.

Land art (which reassembles elements of the natural landscape into sculptural forms) and street art (the bold, often political, usually unsanctioned public art associated with graffiti) are artistic movements that may seem worlds apart. But both reshape shared environments, and both overlap with guerrilla gardening – a creative intervention using plants as paint and streets as canvas. The two movements also merged to inspire the work of artist and guerrilla gardener Melynda Gierard. "Land art," she tells me, "along with textile graffiti, played a huge role in how I got to 'my style' of guerrilla gardening."

This style first emerged in Johannesburg, where Melynda created "biodegradable street art" planters from brightly dyed, text-printed hessian. Today, she guerrilla gardens in Bushwick using

Two of Melynda's creative collaborations: with Poppy Carnation (above) and Lizzy Plapinger (right).

"mostly curb finds" to create colourful street furniture and planters. "This project wouldn't be financially feasible if I weren't using found objects!" she laughs. It's nothing new to her: "Since art school, I've made most of my art from found objects. Now the whole repurpose, reuse, upcycle thing is entering the mainstream. Trash is now everyone's gig because we are burying ourselves in it."

Melynda hopes her work inspires people to explore their own creative potential. "Most people put artistry in a very small box for themselves, but anyone can be super creative. If you're not sure where to start, get experimental!". She encourages everyone to approach growing with the same freedom and fearlessness as she does her art. "For years, I avoided the plant side of things, I just created the art around them. My awakening

came when I started growing from seed. To anyone who thinks they don't have a 'green thumb', just grow a bean in a jar and see! There is growth and potential and learning in seeds, as there is in creativity."

THIS TO THAT: REPURPOSING IDEAS

Wooden cable drum ► Table

Bricks, rocks, or logs ► Bed borders

Railway sleepers ► Low planter edges

Tyre ► Low plant pot

Tyres ► Tall plant pot

Bathtub ► Deep raised bed

Metal headboard ► Trellis

Industrial pallets ► Almost anything!

PROPAGATING PLANTS

Propagation is the process of growing new plants from existing ones. There are lots of ways to propagate plants, including:

» **GROWING FROM SEED**
Growing from seed allows you to witness a plant's full life cycle. You can start seeds in containers indoors, or sow directly into the ground (pages 156–157).

» **ROOTING A CUTTING** Some plants can create roots from the base of a cut stem. E.g. wild clary (*Salvia verbenaca*), common mint (*Mentha spicata*), rose (*Rosa* spp.).

» **DIVIDING THE PLANT** Perennials often form large clusters of small plantlets that can be broken off and planted individually. E.g. bugle (*Ajuga reptans*), primrose (*Primula vulgaris*), yellow iris (*Iris pseudacorus*).

» **REPLANTING OFFSETS** Some plants grow miniature replicas of themselves ("offsets") that can be removed and replanted. E.g. water soldier (*Stratiotes aloides*), biting stonecrop (*Sedum acre*), daffodil (*Narcissus* spp.).

» **AIR ROOTING** Air rooting, or air layering, encourages new roots to form from a stem or branch still attached to the parent plant, by cutting into a bud and wrapping it with damp moss. E.g. fig tree (*Ficus carica*), field maple (*Acer campestre*), common lilac (*Syringa vulgaris*).

Even within these categories, different plants require different variations on the method and seasonal timing, so it's best to research the best way to propagate the plant you have in mind.

SAVING SEEDS

Finding a plant that's gone to seed and knowing you can grow hundreds more from it – for free – always feels like a miracle.

Saving seeds from food and plants is an easy, fun, and rewarding way to grow new life. Not only that, it's a form of resistance against multinational chemical companies' monopolisation of the global seed market, and a way to safeguard seed diversity – which is essential to future-proof food and ecosystems.

HOW TO SEED SAVE

1. Collect seedheads on a dry day, when they're "ripe" (you'll see they've turned from a fleshy green to a dry brown).
2. Place a paper bag around the ripe seedheads and carefully pull (or cut) them off into it. Label the bag.
3. Dry the seedheads out on a tray on a warm windowsill or in an airing cupboard. (For fleshy fruits or berries, press them into a sieve and rinse off the pulp in cold water. Dry the seeds on a paper towel.)
4. Keep dried seeds in a paper packet, labelled with the month, year, and plant type.
5. Place the paper packet(s) inside an airtight container. Add rice to the container to help remove excess moisture (or any silica gel packets you've saved from product boxes), and store in a cool, dark, dry place.

WHERE TO SEED SAVE

» From your own plants and food (especially heirloom varieties).
» From public plants (only take a few pods).
» Swap seeds at a local seed exchange (if you can't find one, organise one!).

IF YOU DO BUY SEEDS

AVOID: HYBRID SEED (F1, F2…)
F1 seeds are created when humans selectively breed two strains of a plant variety to create uniform offspring with particular traits. Seeds saved from the resulting plants (F2 seeds, and so on) won't "grow true" to the parent - each successive generation loses reliability, resilience, yield, looks, and overall quality.

AVOID: GM / GMO SEED
The prevalence of GM (genetically modified) seeds - which are manufactured in labs - threatens the genetic diversity of our food supply.

LOOK FOR: OPEN POLLINATED
"Open" pollination occurs due to natural mechanisms (animals, wind, etc.). Because the flow of pollen isn't controlled or limited, open-pollinated plants are more genetically diverse, and can also adapt to local growing conditions and climate over time.

LOOK FOR: HEIRLOOM / HERITAGE SEED
Seeds that have been saved and passed down for generations (at least 50 years) within a family, community, region, or project. They're well adapted to local conditions, help protect genetic diversity, and usually have better flavour and nutrient density than ones you'll find in a high street DIY store.

Open-pollinated, heirloom seeds cost a little more, but you'll be able to save the next generation's seeds (or let the plants self-seed), and the next - meaning, you'll never have to pay to plant them again!

SOFTWOOD STEM CUTTINGS

This method of propagation, best done in spring or summer, works for many perennials (both hardy and tender), deciduous shrubs and climbers, and some trees.

GET EQUIPPED

Secateurs or scissors (sterilized)

Clear compostable (or plastic) carrier bag

Water spray bottle

Container

Soilless propagation potting mix

Organic rooting hormone (optional)

01.

Find 3 to 5 non-flowering stems from the plant you wish to propagate and cut them near the base. Place in a carrier bag with a spritz of water.

02.

At home, prepare a container for your cuttings to develop roots in, using a soilless propagation potting mix (these contain sand and/or gravel, and allow more air in).

03.

Gently pull the lower leaves off, leaving 2 or 3 at the top.

node →

04.

Find a node (a point with a bud, or where leaves branch from the stem) that's roughly 12.5cm (5in) down from the top of the stem. Make a cut just below this node, at a 45° angle. To encourage root growth, you can dip the cut base into organic rooting hormone.

05.

Push the stem vertically into the potting mix until it stands up – keeping the leaves above the potting mix.

06.

Repeat Steps 3 to 6 for the remaining cuttings, ensuring they're evenly spaced in the pot. Firm the potting mix around them gently and spray thoroughly.

07.

Cover in your clear bag, ensuring it doesn't touch the cuttings. Transfer the covered pot to a warm, humid, light (but out of direct sunlight) indoor spot.

08.

Spray with water often to keep the potting mix evenly moist (but not drenched). After about 2 months, you'll feel resistance when you pull the stem as roots have developed. You can now transfer your cuttings to a new pot with fresh potting soil.

DO THE PLANTING

AIR HORN YOU'VE MADE IT TO THE MAIN EVENT! STRIPPED TO ITS ESSENCE, GUERRILLA GARDENING IS ALL ABOUT THIS STEP: PLANTING.

Guerrilla gardening can involve many forms of action; you may find yourself organising volunteers, building structures, painting, dancing, filming, polemicising, and protesting – perhaps all at once. But, without sowing seeds, planting greenery – creating an abundance of nature where before there was only absence – none of the rest can truly be guerrilla gardening. So, here's how you do it.

GENERAL ADVICE
ROOT DOWN
Whatever you're planting – from new bulb to mature tree – the root end goes down into the soil, and the shoot end (which grows into the plant) faces up.

HARDEN OFF
If you've started plants indoors, whether from seeds or cuttings, you'll need to acclimatise them

to outdoor conditions by gradually increasing their outdoor exposure – a process known as "hardening off". They should be outside in their pots for at least a week before being planted in the ground.

WATER IN
Right after planting, deeply water your plants. This helps them deal with "transplant shock" – the shock of being moved from their previous environment to a new one (plants weren't built to teleport).

LOOK UP
Though there are a few general principles to follow, every species has its own planting requirements, with some needing special processes or conditions. If you want the best chance of success, look up guidance for that specific plant type rather than guessing!

GUERRILLA ADVICE

» **Wet street soil before working into it**. Two reasons for this:

» If the soil is dry, dusty particles of god-knows-what fly up at you. I learnt this tip the hard way, after (one too many times) vigorously breaking apart compacted soil and then wondering where the strong smell of piss had suddenly come from.

» Wetting compacted soil makes it much easier to break apart or rake over (which in turn helps seeds and plants take hold).

» **Wear gloves**. There's always a chance of encountering needles, knives, and other things you don't want to touch in rubbish heaps or bedraggled municipal planting.

» **Wear a hi-vis**. This one's up to you, but they lend an air of authority (or invisibility) that can deter people from questioning you.

ROOT DOWN
SHOOT UP

START WITH SOIL

There's an old gardening adage, "a penny for the plant, a pound for the hole". Meaning, time invested in preparing the ground for planting more than pays off. Healthy gardens start with healthy soil. But city soil is often shitty soil, sun-crisped and compacted – making it difficult for plants to live long or prosper in.

Prepare lifeless soil for planting by adding organic material...

COMPOST

Composting converts organic "waste", like garden cuttings and vegetable peelings, into fertiliser. There are many ways to make compost, and it's something you can do at home (search "bokashi" and "vermiculture"), though there's likely a community compost site near you too! If the soil is truly lifeless, dig compost right through (otherwise, try "No Dig"! *See right*).

Eco Note: *If you buy compost, make sure it's peat-free: peatlands are vital habitats and carbon stores, which are being destroyed to extract peat.*

MANURE

Natural fertiliser made from herbivore animal dung, sometimes with bedding mixed in. Knowing how and where to apply manure depends on which animal it's from (usually horses, cows, or chickens), and how "fresh" or "well-rotted" it is.

It's generally best to apply manure in the late autumn or winter, so it breaks down in time for spring, meaning its high nitrogen content doesn't burn plants.

Eco Note: *Some farmers feed animals herbicide-infused hay. No surprises, this isn't great for growing plants in, so look for organic, herbicide-free manure.*

MULCH

Plant matter spread over the surface of soil to lock in moisture, regulate soil temperature, and suppress unwanted plant growth. Ultimately, it rots down, feeding the soil life and your plants.

Eco Note: *Much of nature's mulch (fallen leaves, broken sticks and the like) gets swept away by council cleaning squads. Spreading mulch on grey, barren city soil is an act of guerrilla gardening that lays the foundations for new life. Try it on tree beds over winter.*

NO DIGGITY

Soil should be a thronging, biodiverse ecosystem. But repeatedly disturbing soil can harm the bacteria, fungi, microbes, and creatures within it. "No Dig" planting reduces soil disturbance, and so maintains healthy soil life. It also helps you plant into soil that's covered by hard-to-budge grass or other rampant, unhelpful plants.

A BASIC GUIDE TO NO DIG GROWING:

Lay down sheets of plain cardboard (with any labels or tape removed). This will block light from reaching plants underneath, killing any unwanted existing growth. If there are any plants you want to keep, cut holes in the card for them to grow through.

Cover the cardboard in a thick layer of peat-free compost.

Plant directly into the compost (you can do this right away), and water everything thoroughly. (You can add a layer of mulch on top, for good measure).

After around 2 months, the cardboard will have broken down and the plant roots should now be growing into the soil below.

GREEN & BLUE ECO CARE

Harlem, New York City

Meet the woman transforming an inner-city esplanade with No Dig pollinator gardens.

When Simone Marques started sowing seeds around the street trees in her East Harlem neighbourhood, people thought she was crazy. "They'd shake their heads and laugh, "*Dios te bendiga*" [God bless you]. They thought the flowers would just get destroyed." But, to everyone's surprise (including Simone's), they flourished. "People would stop by, take photos, chat – it created a rare-found sense of community in this metropolis."

This was a serendipitous side-effect of her personal mission: helping the Big Apple's bees. "I'd been hearing 'save the bees' and 'insect extinction', and thought I could help a little." After starting small, and succeeding, she was ready to make a bigger splash. "One thing bugging me (no pun intended!) was the lack of pollinator-friendly flowers on our riverfront."

She decided to connect her newly formed community gardening group, Green & Blue Eco Care, with other local organisations, including one dedicated to improving the East Manhattan riverfront. Together, they created a perennial pollinator garden, paid for by donations. This blooming marvellous achievement gave Simone the courage to go on to create her own *guerrilla* garden along the esplanade. "Guerrilla gardening gave me the freedom to play by my own rules, and go about things informally."

"With the first garden, we stumbled onto the No Dig method out of necessity; when we turned up to the spot we'd found (and were told would be prepared) it was covered in grass! The cardboard was a way to remediate that." The happy accident led to Simone adopting the minimally disruptive approach for her next

"I'M A BIG BELIEVER THAT TOGETHER IS BETTER."
Simone Marques

guerrilla garden. With the help of 30 volunteers, she covered a strip of the East River promenade in cardboard, healthy soil, and drought tolerant, native flowers – naturally, without pesticides or herbicides. And she didn't stop there. "This year we created our second pollinator garden. On both occasions, we had bees and butterflies inspecting the flowers before we had even transplanted them! They really need these spaces."

PLANTING BULBS

Bulbs are a simple yet impactful guerrilla gardening medium. Their stems and flowers take up hardly any space, so can be easily tucked in among other plants (or even layered on top of each other), they're easy to plant, and there are different bulbs in bloom almost all year round.

GET EQUIPPED

True bulbs or corms

Dibber or bulb planter
(depending on size)

Bulb starter (optional)

01.

Grab a handful of bulbs and scatter onto your chosen spot, to get a natural-looking spread. Make sure there's a distance of at least one bulb's-width between them.

02.

Where they lay, use your dibber (for small bulbs and corms) or bulb planter (for larger ones) to make a hole in the ground three times as deep as the bulb is tall.

03.

Optional: Scatter in some bulb starter. It contains mycorrhizal fungi, which encourages root development.

04.

Put the bulb in the hole with its pointed "nose" facing upwards, and the roots, downwards.

05.

Cover back up with soil (if you used a bulb planter, this will be perfectly cut out for you), and gently firm the soil down.

06.

Water well.

Plant spring-flowering bulbs in autumn, and summer-flowering bulbs in spring.

RIGHT BULB MOMENT

Gardeners use the term "bulb" to refer to a range of underground plant parts that store nutrients to allow the plant to regrow each year. Knowing which of these you're dealing with can help you find out how best to plant it.

TRUE BULBS Onion-like (or literally an onion), true bulbs are characteristically layered, and usually have a papery outer skin. E.g. daffodil (*Narcissus* spp.).

CORMS Corms are modified stem bases that look very like bulbs, with a thicker, wider root base. E.g. crocus (*Crocus* spp.).

TUBERS Tubers form at the base of a (normal) root, so you can get several tubers from one plant. They each have several buds (or "eyes"), so you can also get several plants from one tuber. E.g. potato (*Solanum tuberosum*).

TUBEROUS ROOTS Tuberous roots are modified, exaggerated plant roots, which form around a plant's central stem. E.g. dahlia (*Dahlia* spp.).

RHIZOMES Thick, horizontally growing underground stems that develop buds along this underground length, which can grow into individual plants. E.g. wavy-leaved rhubarb (*Rheum rhabarbarum*).

PLANTING POTTED PLANTS

Garden plants are typically traded in pots. If you're planting potted plants in your guerrilla garden, here are a few tips to help you get it right:

FIXING BOUND ROOTS

Potted plants are often found "pot-bound" or "root-bound", meaning their roots have outgrown the pot and become a dense, tight mass. To fix this:

» Shake or tap the rootball to loosen and release some of the soil.

» Carefully tease the clump of roots apart (in the same way you'd detangle hair); start with the lowest areas and work up.

 » Be as gentle as you can, but don't worry if some roots break – it's better for the plant to grow new ones out into the soil than be root-bound.

PLANTING IN THE GROUND

01.

Dig a hole slightly wider than the plant pot, but no deeper. To check this, place the pot in the hole: the top of the potting compost should be level with the ground, and you should be able to fit your index finger between the pot and the side of the hole all the way around.

02.

Remove the plant from its pot (teasing apart the roots if needed and allowing any loose soil to fall into the hole) and place it into the ground.

PLANTING PLUG PLANTS

Plug plants are young plants that can be ordered in the post. They're a win-win for new growers: cheaper than mature plants, but faster and more straightforward than growing from seed.

Simple tips for plug plants:

» Be gentle with plug plants – push them out of the containers they arrive in by putting a pencil into the soil and sliding them out. If you have to, only handle their top two leaves.

» Smaller plugs will need to be repotted in an appropriately sized pot with compost mix (use a dibber or your finger to make the hole), cared for indoors, then hardened off for at least a week before being planted out.

» Larger, "garden ready" plugs can be planted out right away, if the weather is warm enough.

» Water plugs before and after transplanting and planting.

03.

Fill any gaps underneath and around the plant with compost, so it sits tightly surrounded by earth and level with the ground surface. Water deeply.

PLANTING IN CONTAINERS

01.

Position the plant – still in its pot – into the planter.

02.

Pack compost around it firmly. This will create a perfectly sized and shaped hole for your plant.

03.

Remove the plant from its pot (teasing apart the roots if needed and allowing any loose soil to fall into the hole) and place it in the compost.

04.

Add any extra compost in as needed, ensuring it doesn't build up around the stem, and firm down. Water deeply.

PLANTING TREES

Trees and bushes typically come "bare root", meaning they've been taken clean out of the soil or compost they were growing in. Here's how to plant a bare-root tree (the same applies for other bare-root plants, minus the wooden stake and tie).

GET EQUIPPED

Tree

Bin bag

Large bucket

Spade

Bamboo cane

Garden fork

Wooden stake

Mallet

Buckle tie and spacer

TREE TIPS

Avoid planting too deeply, or in too narrow a hole: 90% of all young tree deaths are attributable to these mistakes. Unless the soil is mostly sand, or of terrible quality, don't fill the hole with compost. Doing so will only encourage the roots to stay in this fertile "comfort zone" rather than reaching out and down for nutrients (and so growing stronger).

01.

As soon as you get the tree, find the soil "tide mark" on the root flare: the dark residue at the base of the trunk left by soil it was previously planted in. This is your guide for how deep to plant your woody friend.

02.

In the lead-up to planting, keep the tree's roots moist, shaded, and protected from wind, by covering them in a bin bag or opaque sheet, or submerging them in a pile of compost (up to the tide mark).

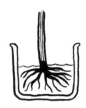

03.

About an hour before planting, submerge the tree's roots in a bucket of water – keeping the tide mark a bit above water level.

04.

While you're soaking the roots, dig a hole wide enough for them to fit into without bending, and deep enough so that the tide mark will be level with the ground surface. Check this depth by placing a bamboo cane across the hole, and lowering the tree in, to see if the tide mark comes level with it.

05.

Look at the root pattern and work out the best place for the stake to go in. It should be about 2.5cm (1in) from the tree, at a 45° angle.

06.

Loosen the sides of your hole with a garden fork to make it easier for the roots to grow and spread.

07.

Have a friend hold the tree upright in the centre of the hole while you backfill it with the soil you've just dug up. Ensure you thoroughly fill between the roots, leaving no air bubbles.

08.

Once the hole is filled, firm it down with your heel (or a spade if you can't do this) and water deeply. Check the soil level again, and fill in any dips or gaps.

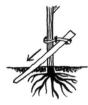

09.

Drive the wooden stake in, 2.5cm (1in) from the tree, at a 45° angle, taking care not to bash into any roots.

10.

Secure the stake to the tree with the buckle tie and a spacer.

Check in on your tree, water it, and loosen the tie as it grows. Spread mulch around the base, leaving a 10cm (4in) gap around the trunk.

THE ROUNDABOUT GARDEN CLASSROOM

Stoke Newington, London

How trees, shrubs, bulbs, seeds, and containers created an inclusive, immersive garden classroom.

The south side of Newington Green roundabout had been neglected for a decade. At one edge, spooky and spiderwebbed, sat a long-abandoned council gardeners' hut, "surrounded by dying plants, rubbish, and dog poo".

Just ten minutes away, in a secluded garden, Marnie Rose's charity The Garden Classroom (TGC) was leading nature learning sessions. "TGC is about social justice," Marnie says, "it's about making nature accessible for everyone. Our priority is – and always will be – to reach disadvantaged groups."

Unfortunately, the spaces they operated in were closed off from the public. "Islington has the lowest amount of open-access green space per person in England," she tells me. But there was a space the borough was failing to use: the large untended

area surrounding the deserted hut. You can guess what happened next. Marnie took over the space and transformed the hut into TGC headquarters – with the council eagerly handing over the keys. "They practically bit our hand off!" she says. "They knew about our work across the borough, and had no budget to do anything with the space themselves... both sides knew it would've remained ignored if TGC hadn't intervened."

With gardeners Lizzy Cook and Ruth Ferguson, Marnie transformed the sad, tangled "municipal planting" (a term she dryly uses as a pejorative) into a thriving nature classroom. As we walk around the space, she points out leaves that follow the Fibonacci sequence, berry trees, and bat boxes. Landscape designer Ruth explains: "We put local children at the heart of the design process. They wanted a book corner, so we used a natural circle in the trees to make a storytelling circle. We started with zero budget; everything you see was either donated, or paid for by donations."

The roundabout garden proves councils aren't always a guerrilla gardener's nemesis. At no point did Islington Council interfere, intervene, or otherwise impede the group's work; they stood back and let them grow. "Trust opens many doors!" Marnie advises. "Councils are waking up to the benefits of community-led greening. As long as it's done safely and competently, they shouldn't stand in your way."

"WE'RE JUST LOCAL PEOPLE WHO SAID, 'WELL THAT'S DEAD, LET'S TURN IT INTO SOMETHING PEOPLE WILL ENJOY!' AND WE DID."

Marnie Rose

DIRECT SOWING

Guerrilla sowing – sowing in the streets – is a form of what's called "direct sowing": sowing seeds straight into the ground (rather than starting them in pots indoors and transferring them outside later). Loads of hardy flowers and vegetables can be sown outdoors, and many even prefer it.

While you can start plants off indoors, direct sowing is more straightforward, and means you don't have to turn half your kitchen into a seedling nursery.

PREP

Loosen the surface of the soil. It's best to use a proper garden fork or rake, but when guerrilla gardening you may need to get creative and simply use what's to hand, whether that's a stick or a spork.

SPACE

Find out how much space your seedlings need to have between them and scatter your seeds (or create holes) according to that spacing.

Don't sow too thickly: plants need adequate room to grow to full size. *Eco Note: Traditional gardening guides advise intentionally sowing too densely, then "thinning" the resulting seedlings (pulling out all but the strongest few), which to me seems like a waste of time and healthy plants.*

DEPTH

Generally speaking, the smaller a seed is, the shallower it should be sown. Some of the tiniest seeds shouldn't be covered at all, or only by a light scattering of horticultural sand (as they need light to germinate).

LIVE & DIRECT

As a rule of thumb, plant seeds in a hole twice as deep as the seed is wide (or cover them in compost to that depth). That said, always check the packet, or look up the ideal depth for the variety you're sowing.

TIMING

Seeds need different temperatures and weather conditions to germinate. Some seeds need to be sown in autumn, as they won't germinate unless they've first experienced winter cold; others (namely half-hardy annuals) must be sown in late spring, after all danger of frost has passed. Check seed packets (or search online) for the best months to sow that seed in.

WATER

Water the seeds gently (don't slosh a bucket over them). If you can, use a watering can – specifically, one fitted with a sprinkler head (called a "rose") – or create your own using a plastic bottle (page 165).

Eco Note: *My top tip for guerrilla sowing is to do it just before (or while) it rains. That way, you can sow far and wide without having to lug water around. Plus, you'll be saving water!*

MAKE SEED BOMBS

These subtle, pocketable pellets are a staple in the guerrilla gardener's arsenal, letting you grow on the go. There's no need for tools, gloves, or dirty knees; just throw them onto exposed soil as you make your way around town, and let sunshine and rainfall take care of the rest.

GET EQUIPPED

Measuring cup

Red clay powder

Mixing bowl

Water

Fork

Peat-free seed compost

Native wildflower seeds

Cardboard box

01.

Tip about ½ a cup of clay powder into the mixing bowl. Keep some extra to one side, as you may need it again in a minute (to get the right consistency).

02.

Add a dash of water and mix into the clay with the fork to form a paste.

03.

Add about 2 cups of compost and mix it thoroughly with the clay. It's easiest to use the fork at first, then your hands.

04.

Check the structure of the mix. Will it form a ball? If not, you may need to add more clay, or more water. If it's holding a ball too solidly, add more compost.

» Bear in mind: too much clay, and the balls won't break apart when used; too much water, and the seeds are more likely to start germinating too soon (plus the mix will be messier to work with).

05.

Once you're happy with the texture of your "dough", it's time to carefully mix the seeds through. Try to spread them as evenly throughout as you can.

06.

Take small lumps of the mixture and ball it into spheres, each around 2.5cm (1in) in diameter.

» That said, they can really be any size and don't even have to be balls! If you're feeling brave, try making cubes, hearts, or pyramids – you could even make a sculpture.

07.

As you make them, pop your seed bombs into a cardboard box. When you're done, close the lid, and leave in a warm (but not hot), dry place to dry out. The smaller they are, the faster they'll dry, but it should be about a day or two.

In the spring and autumn, keep a bowl of seed bombs by the door to grab as you head out, so you're armed to do your good seed for the day.

PROVIDE & PROTECT

A GARDEN IS AN ENDLESS STORY, CO-WRITTEN BY NATURE AND GARDENER. DON'T LET YOUR GUERRILLA GARDEN WIND UP A SHORT STORY WITH A TRAGIC ENDING.

Once you've created your pocket paradise, safeguard it. All gardeners are really guardians. For *guerrilla* gardeners, this guardianship extends beyond routine watering, mulching, pruning, and so on, to include protection against active assailants. Whether it's the council's glyphosate unit, or CAVE people (Citizens Against Virtually Everything), there may be someone out to destroy what you've created.

This final step of the guerrilla gardening process involves **CULTIVATION** and **COMMUNICATION**...

CULTIVATION

There are entire books dedicated to how to care for a garden, and it is at this juncture that I must pass the baton on to them. I'll leave you with some starting tips though:

» **FINE TUNING** Observe how your garden's various elements are developing over time to work out how to keep it flourishing overall. Is something becoming too dominant? Are there gaps that could be filled? Does the soil need nourishment?

THIS IS WHY WE CAN'T HAVE NICE THINGS

Three (tragically) true stories illustrating the kind of thinking you may need to defend your garden from:
» An audience member in a talk I once gave (about the need for urban nature) complained that we shouldn't be making cities greener because some people have hayfever.
» A fellow nature-lover told me their housing estate had banished all flowering plants from the grounds in case they attracted bees, which "could sting someone".
» Incredible Edible Leigh-On-Sea's residential street corner guerrilla garden was destroyed by the phantom landowner, who then bafflingly (or tauntingly) covered the spot in plastic grass.

» **HEALTH CHECK** Look for signs of disease by checking leaves for telltale symptoms: spots, mildew, and lumps. Search these symptoms to diagnose the underlying cause and how it could affect that plant, and others around it. Don't rip things out at the first sign of disease, but (if it's serious) this is one valid reason – along with finding an invasive species – to remove a plant.
» **YEAR-ROUND TASKS** Whatever the time of year, there's always gardening that can be done. It can feel like a lot when you're new to gardening, but take it easy by looking up what to do in the present month and enjoy the season's rhythms.

WISE WATERING

» **WHEN?** The best time to water your garden is in the early morning (or evening), as water evaporates slower when the sun is low.

» **WHERE?** Water plants at the base to ensure the water goes deep into the soil, and won't evaporate too quickly. Avoid watering leaves, as (for some plants) it can cause disease.

» **HOW?** Soak the ground thoroughly to encourage deep, strong root growth. (A weekly drench is better than a daily dribble!) Pour the water out slowly – too quick and it's more likely to run off rather than sink in.

Guerrilla Watering Tips

» Fill up close to the site by looking out for a public water fountain or a building maintenance hose tap, or by asking a nearby cafe if they'd mind filling up your watering can.

» If you have a group, make a watering rota to share the responsibility and ownership of the garden.

» Save water by working with nature: collect rainfall in buckets, or design a system to angle it towards your garden.

BOTTLE IT

This has to be the simplest, cheapest makeshift watering can out there. All you need is a plastic bottle (any size) and a corkscrew.

HOW TO TURN A PLASTIC BOTTLE INTO A WATERING CAN

1. Remove the bottle cap and place it right-way-up (i.e. with the flat bit held up by the sides) on a sturdy, solid surface.

2. Hold it by the sides with your non-dominant hand to keep it still.

3. With your dominant hand, use a corkscrew (or bradawl if you have one) to poke several evenly spaced holes into the lid.

4. Screw the cap back on, and hey presto!

Any time you want to use it, remove the lid, fill it up, lid back on, and be on your merry way.

If you want to throw it into a backpack, full, without the water leaking everywhere, just find another plastic bottle lid that's the same size (without holes in) and pop it on. Chuck the holey lid in the bag too and swap it over when you're ready to get watering.

COMMUNICATION

CAMPAIGNS

You may have to campaign to keep your garden alive – or to change the very rules against its existence. Here's a simple step-by-step to crafting your campaign strategy:

1. **WHO** are the key players?
   - » **The Opponent.** Who is opposing your garden? Why?
   - » **The Authority.** Who ultimately decides whether or not your garden stays? Is it the same as the Opponent, or another power? If the Authority is the local council, which person (or people) specifically within that organisation?
   - » **Potential Allies.** Who – in your community and beyond – has a valuable, impactful voice that the Authority will listen to?

2. **WHY** would...
   - » **The Opponent** drop their opposition? How might you incentivise them? They may just want to feel heard, and included. Is there a compromise to be made?

   - » **The Authority** rule in your favour? This can include: wanting to look good (or not wanting to be publicly shamed); not wanting to expend time, money, and resources fighting against a tenacious defence campaign; wanting to reach their community and environmental targets for the area.
   - » **Potential Allies** want to help? What will they get out of it? Why might a win for the garden b e a win for them too?

3. **WHAT** do you need to do to get the desired result?
   - » From petitions to sit-ins, there's a wealth of tactics to consider. You may rally around your garden with a megaphone and placards. You might even "lock-on" to it. Or the best route could simply be getting everyone in the area to email the relevant local councillor.

KNOW YOUR RIGHTS

In the event of police intervention – either while you're guerrilla gardening, or campaigning to protect your garden – follow these precautions:

1. **NO COMMENT** You're not legally obliged to answer police questions. Be wary: even in seemingly informal chats, they may be trying to gather information from you.

2. **NO PERSONAL DETAILS** You don't have to provide your name, address, or date of birth. That said, if you're actually taken into a police station, you may wish to do so to speed your release.

3. **UNDER WHAT POWER?** Police often count on you not knowing the law to get you to comply with their demands. If a police officer orders you to do something, ask: "Under what power?" Make note of what they say.

4. **NO DUTY SOLICITOR** There will be a free solicitor on duty at the police station, but they may not be the best person to help you. Save the numbers of (free) solicitors on your phone that you can contact (page 175).

5. **NO CAUTION** Do not accept a caution unless your solicitor advises it. Doing so is an admission of guilt, and police use this to get you to admit guilt for an offence without having to charge you, provide evidence, or convince a court jury.

Always make a note of the officer's badge and shoulder numbers so you can identify them later.

ANTI-HERBICIDE

```
Guerrilla gardening a bare spot is futile
if it's bare because herbicides - chemicals
designed to kill "pest" plants, i.e. "weeds"
- are regularly sprayed there. Annoying, yes.
But commonly used herbicides (like glyphosate)
cause even bigger problems than that: from
harming bees to humans. Beyond avoiding them
yourself, campaign for these toxic products not
to be used in your area (page 174).
```

THE RON FINLEY PROJECT

South Central Los Angeles, USA

The fashion designer whose fight against food deserts hit international news – and changed LA law.

Ron Finley was sick of two problems in his neighbourhood: the total lack of fresh food ("I call it a food prison"), and the litter-strewn, lifeless road verges. So, in 2010, he picked up a shovel and turned a 150-foot-long strip of soil into an abundant allotment, bursting with sunflowers, kale, and pomegranates.

As a reward, Los Angeles authorities wrote a warrant for his arrest. Ron was appalled. "You abandon this street, yet when I improve it, suddenly you're paying attention? You're not doing anything to bring healthy food to this community, now you want to stop us from doing it ourselves? And you call *me* the criminal? Fuck you!"

Ron rallied his community around the cause and before long his story had been picked up by global news

outlets. The LA authorities "got embarrassed as hell". As a result, Ron not only won his case, but got the law changed. "Now," he shrugs, sitting in the abandoned pool he's turned into an urban jungle, "anyone in Los Angeles can plant food in a parkway."

This win proves Ron's belief that people have the power to affect change, if they choose to. As he says: "You want the planet changed for the better? You change it. We already know they aren't going to change it for us. People say, 'the system is broken'? The system works perfectly! It's designed to keep people down, to keep people in poverty. If they wanted healthy food in these places, they would put healthy food in these places. We have to do it ourselves."

To realise this vision of residents transforming food deserts into food

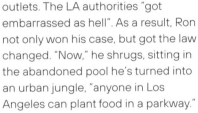

"GROWING YOUR OWN FOOD IS LIKE PRINTING YOUR OWN MONEY."

Ron Finley

sanctuaries, Ron founded the Ron Finley Project, an organisation helping communities see their potential for food growing and self-sufficiency. Ultimately, he says, "the work isn't just about food, it's about freedom. Growing food is a gateway to realising your power."

When I ask if he has any parting advice, he raises an eyebrow and points to his t-shirt. It reads: *Plant. Some. Shit.*

CONVERSATIONS WITH FIENDS

As you set about planting, or subsequently tending your garden, people will sidle over to see what you're up to. 99% of the time, they'll be kind, curious folk who want to thank you, or offer help. Occasionally, however, they'll be bastards.

Here are a few tips on how to deal with them:

» **Kill 'em with kindness.** Always treat people as though they have good intentions (even when they're a scowling, fist-shaking Dickensian villain). Greet them with a smile, be welcoming, and don't get defensive.

» **Confidence is key.** There's a reason "con" is short for "confidence": calm assuredness makes almost anything sound convincing. There's no need to act cagey – remember, you're doing a good deed.

» **Look the part.** Having leaflets, matching t-shirts, a website, or social profile helps make things look "official".

TWO EARS, ONE MOUTH

The really mature thing to do is to listen more than you talk. When the Garden of Earthly Delights II was being created "two people kept complaining about things that simply made no sense," Seng says. "We realised they were probably upset about something else, like feeling excluded. We invited them to the garden, broke bread (well, watermelon), and listened. After that, the problem just disappeared! People often just want to feel seen, and be heard."

- » **Work in broad daylight.**
  Guerrilla gardening at night only invites more suspicion and suggests that what you're doing is mischievous (it is, but don't let them know that!).
- » **Tell the truth, but not the whole truth (so help you God).**
  - » Saying, "We're guerrilla gardening to stick two fingers up to state incompetence and claim our right to grow", won't go down well with everyone.
  - » Instead try: "We're volunteers, tasked with greening this spot." You don't have to say who tasked you. Or, if they probe into it, say "a local community organisation responsible for making the area greener". Again, no need to admit this group is you, or that you've claimed responsibility yourselves.

Regarding the elder in his community who took over the Hope Garden, Tayshan (pictured) says: "We had our differences, but quickly realised there's no sense fighting amongst ourselves – the people in power are laughing if you do that!"

- » **Bore them to death.** If you want someone to stop asking questions, answer in excruciatingly banal detail. For instance...
  "What on earth are you doing?!"
  "Well, you see, first we're picking up this compost, composed of carbon-rich office waste and nitrogen-rich kitchen waste, using flat-blade digging spades, and spreading it onto a 2-metre-squared area. Then..."
  They'll be waiting for the first break in your dull, long-winded ramble to say, "Thanks!" and scarper.
- » **"Misinterpret" their interest.**
  You can also get solipsistic squawkers to leave by thanking them profusely for their interest and inviting them to join in. Hand them a bin bag and gesture at all the litter they can help collect. They'll suddenly remember they have somewhere to be.

Anyone can be the group's designated spokesperson, but people from privileged demographics should consider stepping up to take on potentially thorny conversations (page 15).

SIGNS

Signs signal intention and commitment behind the garden, and so prompt people not to harm it. They can communicate:

1. **WHAT TO DO** E.g. "Please water me", "Help yourself", "Sign our petition".

2. **WHAT NOT TO DO** E.g. "Don't spray glyphosate here", "Not a toilet".

3. **WHAT'S GOING ON** Signs can also act as propaganda. In letting people know how the garden came into being, we can help others – from community members to council staff – see guerrilla gardening's potential and positive impact.

LET'S GROW

Guerrilla gardening is not a silver bullet to the crises we find ourselves in, but it reminds us that we are not powerless.

In creating a guerrilla garden, you plant a seed of a happier, healthier, fairer future. Some of these seeds may fail; others will grow, pollinate, and spread out - who knows how far. Like determined wildflowers pushing up through paving, the movement will crop up wherever colour and life are lacking.

Ready to be on the right side of history?
Get guerrilla gardening.

RESOURCES

GET GOING

» **Guerrilla Gardening Guides & Workshops** *dreamgreen.earth*
» **How to Join Park(ing) Day** *myparkingday.org/how-to*
» **How to Depave** *depave.org/resources/how-to-depave*
» **Anti-Herbicide Campaign Materials**
  » UK: *pan-uk.org/make-my-town-pesticide-free/*
  » ROI: *pan-europe.info/*
  » Global: *pan-international.org/*
» **Get Funding**
  » Crowdfunding for community-led local improvement *spacehive.com*
  » Grants for guerrilla action *guerrillafoundation.org*
  » Find local community organisations *gov.uk/find-a-community-support-group-or-organisation*

GET EQUIPPED

» **Free Plants** *wayward.co.uk*
» **Free Seeds** *cultivatingchange.co.uk* or *seedsaving.network*
» **Free Compost** *makesoil.org* or *sharewaste.com*
» **Lending Libraries** *ethicalconsumer.org/home-garden/library-things-directory*
» **Organic, Ethical Seed Suppliers** *vitalseeds.co.uk* or *realseeds.co.uk* or *seedcooperative.org.uk*

GET INFORMED

» **Find Plants to Suit Your Site** *rhs.org.uk/plants/search-form* or *gardenia.net/plant-finder*
» **Native Plant Lists**
  » UK: *gardenia.net/native-plants/united-kingdom*
  » ROI: *en.wikipedia.org/wiki/Flora_of_Ireland*
» **Invasive Plant Lists**
  » UK & ROI: *rhs.org.uk/prevention-protection/invasive-non-native-plants*
  » Government Advice
    » England & Wales: *gov.uk/guidance/invasive-non-native-alien-plant-species-rules-in-england-and-wales*
    » Scotland: *gov.scot/policies/wildlife-management/invasive-non-native-species*
    » Northern Ireland: *daera-ni.gov.uk/articles/eu-invasive-alien-species*
    » ROI: *invasives.ie/what-can-i-do*
» **Hardiness Zones**
  » RHS Hardiness Ratings *rhs.org.uk/plants/trials-awards/award-of-garden-merit/rhs-hardiness-rating*
  » USDA Hardiness Ratings
    » UK: *plantmaps.com/interactive-united-kingdom-plant-hardiness-zone-map-celsius.php*
    » ROI: *plantmaps.com/interactive-ireland-plant-hardiness-zone-map-celsius.php*

- » **Know Your Rights**
  - » Legal Advice for Protesters
    - » *informeddissent.info*
    - » *greenandblackcross.org/action/know-your-rights/*
  - » Protest Solicitors' Numbers
    informeddissent.info/bustcard
  - » Stop & Search
    - » England & Wales: *gov.uk/police-powers-to-stop-and-search-your-rights*
    - » Scotland: *mygov.scot/police-stop-search*
    - » Northern Ireland: *psni.police.uk/about-us/our-initiatives/stop-and-search*
    - » ROI: *iccl.ie/wp-content/uploads/2017/11/ICCL_KYR_Justice_2014_LR.pdf*

GET READING

- » Alinsky, Saul D., *Rules For Radicals: A Pragmatic Primer for Realistic Radicals*, Vintage Books, 1989.
- » Carter, Majora, *Reclaiming Your Community: You Don't Have to Move out of Your Neighborhood to Live in a Better One*, Berrett-Koehler Publishers, 2022.
- » Dowding, Charles, *No Dig: Nurture Your Soil to Grow Better Veg with Less Effort*, DK, 2022.
- » Lamborn Wilson, Peter and Weinberg, Bill (eds.), *Avant Gardening: Ecological Struggle in the City and the World*, Autonomedia, 1999.
- » McKay, George, *Radical Gardening: Politics, Idealism and Rebellion in the Garden*, Frances Lincoln, 2011.
- » Miles, Ellen (ed.), *Nature is a Human Right: Why We're Fighting for Green in a Grey World*, DK, 2022.
- » Reynolds, Richard, *On Guerrilla Gardening: A Handbook for Gardening without Boundaries*, Bloomsbury Publishing, 2008.
- » Rosa, Marcos L. and Weiland, Ute E. (eds.), *Handmade Urbanism: From Community Initiatives to Participatory Models*, JOVIS Verlag, 2019.
- » Smaje, Chris, *A Small Farm Future: Making the Case for a Society Built Around Local Economies, Self-Provisioning, Agricultural Diversity, and a Shared Earth*, Chelsea Green Publishing, 2020.
- » Tracey, David, *Guerrilla Gardening: A Manualfesto*, New Society Publishers, 2007.
- » Walton, Samantha, *Everybody Needs Beauty: In Search of the Nature Cure*, Bloomsbury Circus, 2021.
- » Warhurst, Pam and Sikking, Anne, *INCREDIBLE EDIBLE Seeds to Solutions: The Power of Small Actions*, Incredible Edible CIC, 2021.

GLOSSARY

Annual plants Plants that germinate, produce leaves, stems, and flowers, set seed, and die – all within a single year.

Biennial plants Plants with a two-year life cycle: in year one, they germinate and grow; in year two, they flower, set seed, and die down.

Brownfield site An area of land previously built upon, which has since been left vacant.

Civic Related to an area's administration or governing body; municipal.

Commons Areas of land treated as a shared resource, collectively managed by the people.

Deciduous A woody plant that loses its leaves in autumn and sprouts new ones in spring.

Eco-fascism Using environmentalism as a pretext for fascist viewpoints. The phrase "humans are the virus", and citing "overpopulation" (especially in the Global South) as the root cause of climate and ecological concerns, are examples.

Evergreen A woody plant that keeps its leaves all year round.

Food desert An area where access to fresh food is extremely limited or non-existent.

Grafting Placing a cutting of one plant (scion or bud) into or on a stem, root, or branch of another (stock) to create a union that continues to grow.

Grassroots Grassroots movements rely on self-mobilising groups driving the change they want to see from the ground up. In grassroots action, a group of people who care about a particular cause (often personal to them and taking place in their area) harness their local knowledge and shared skills to solve it together.

Greyification The ongoing smothering of our planet's vibrant natural carpet with hard inorganic surfacing in various shades of grey (concrete, tarmac, paving slabs, asphalt, gravel, and so on).

Guerrilla (n.) A member of a small, independent group taking part in autonomous, irregular combat against a larger, more formal power.

WHAT'S IN A NAME?

Guerrilla (which literally translates as "small war") is a diminutive of the Spanish word *guerra* ("war"). The term was coined in the early 19th century when small, independent groups of Spanish and Portuguese rebel fighters, known as *guerrilleros*, helped defend the Iberian Peninsula against Napoleon's Grande Armée.

The word then experienced something of a renaissance in the 20th century, when it was adopted by the likes of Mao Zedong - who named his 1937 military handbook 论游击战 [lun you ji zhan] or *"On Guerrilla Warfare"* - and Che Guevara, whose 1960 answer to Mao's tactical tome is titled *La Guerra de Guerrillas*, or *"Guerrilla Warfare"*.

Since then, "guerrilla" has evolved to denote agile, impromptu, unauthorised actions of various sorts.

Despite its blood-soaked etymology, guerrilla gardening is all about creating life...

Guerrilla garden (v.) To cultivate plants in a public space, without civic interference.

Guerrilla garden (n.) A public garden (large or small) created by autonomous grassroots action.

Hardiness A measure of how well a plant can survive extreme climatic conditions. In the UK, "hardy" plants are those that can survive cold winters; in arid climates, the term refers to plants that can withstand heat and drought.

Invasive species These species' adaptations make them highly vigorous and prolific when introduced to a new environment, meaning they can crowd out other species, and imbalance the surrounding ecosystem. So-called "invasive species" are not inherently "invasive". Rather, they become so as a result of human meddling. For instance, Japanese knotweed (*Reynoutria japonica*) is not invasive in its native Japan, where natural predators and competitors help keep it under control. After Victorians introduced it to the UK, however, it swiftly became invasive. As well as being relocated, species can become invasive if their surrounding environment is degraded in a way that gives them a competitive advantage.

Meanwhile site Any space – from a vacant lot or brownfield site to a building or empty shop unit – that is awaiting long-term, fixed-use, or development (which may be known or speculative), which can be used temporarily while it is empty.

Native species Species that are indigenous to the region they are found in, and naturally evolved into being there, without human intervention.

Naturalised species A species is said to have "naturalised" when it has been brought to a new, non-native environment, then successfully adapted to it: growing, reproducing, and otherwise establishing a self-sustaining population, without human cultivation.

Organic gardening Gardening that enriches the entire garden ecosystem (including soil and wildlife) – not just plants. This means ditching manufactured chemical fertilisers and pesticides, and embracing a holistic, nature-led approach.

Perennial plants Perennial plants have long-lasting roots that survive through the seasons, allowing the plant to grow back, year after year. Herbaceous perennials die down to the ground in autumn and regrow in spring; evergreen perennials keep their leaves all year round.

Pesticides Chemical substances – including insecticides, herbicides, and fungicides – engineered to kill living organisms considered "pests" to cultivated plants.

Recommoning The activity or political philosophy of returning land to commons. In reclaiming public land for public good, guerrilla gardening is a form of recommoning.

Seedhead The dried flowering or fruiting part of a plant that contains seeds.

Tenants and Residents Association (TRA or TARA) A formal, voluntary group of local residents who seek to improve their neighbourhood by representing and reflecting the community's needs and interests.

Tree beds Also known as tree pits, these are the soil-filled breaks in hard paving in which a street tree is planted.

Weed "Weed" isn't a botanical classification – it's a judgement: "You are in the wrong place". Many species that society has decided are "weeds" are actually medicinal, edible, habitat-providing, nectar-creating, soil-enriching wonders.

Wildflower Annual or perennial flowering plants that grow naturally in the wild (meaning they're ancient species that haven't been genetically modified and tend to be self-seeded).

NOTES

INTRODUCTION (PP.06–27)

08   "Nature is a Human Right, a campaign for the United Nations to recognise access to healthy, green environments as a human right": Find out more and join the movement at natureisahumanright.earth

08   "inequalities highlighted (and exacerbated) at the time": In lower-income areas of London (where residents often don't have a garden), people flocked to public parks as much-needed mental and physical welfare resources. In response, short-sighted councils closed these busier parks, resulting in a caricature of green space inequality: while people in wealthy areas could access both public and private green space, poorer groups were shut out from nature entirely.

09   "I came across... guerrilla gardening": I particularly remember watching Ron Finley's 2013 TED Talk – *Ron Finley: A guerrilla gardener in South Central LA*, TED, 2013, ted.com/talks/ron_finley_a_guerrilla_ gardener_in_south_central_la

11   "our habitats impact our health and happiness": If you, like me, are interested in how the greenness (or greyness) of our surroundings impacts our wellbeing, you may be pleased to know I've edited an anthology of powerful, accessible writing – from global scientists, artists, and activists – on this very subject. See: Miles, E. (ed.), *Nature is a Human Right*, DK, 2022, in particular the "Welfare"chapter, pp.28–103.

11   "'using plants to reclaim public space for the public good'": Tracey, D., *Guerrilla Gardening: A Manualfesto*, New Society Publishers, 2007, p.1.

12   "Paris offers citizens a 'permis de végétaliser'": "Le permis de végétaliser", paris.fr, June 2022.

12   "Los Angeles allows residents to plant, *without* a permit, in the parkways directly outside their houses": City of Los Angeles, "Residential Parkway Landscaping Guidelines", Office of the Board of Public Works, June 2015, streetsla.lacity.org/sites/ default/files/Residential_Parkway_Landscaping_ Guidelines.pdf

12   "East London's Hackney council took a public stance of allowing residents to plant in tree beds in 2021": Based on my own conversations with the council, in which they provided me with a list of tree beds in the area that they said residents could plant in – though I didn't find this advertised publicly.

13   "Graffiti artist Banksy's work ceased to be 'vandalism' years ago": Perrin, I., "This is how much value Banksy murals add to your home", readingchronicle.co.uk, March 2021.

14   "projects to 'green' scrap land have led to drops in gun violence, vandalism, and burglaries": In New Haven, Connecticut (a city whose crime rate is twice the United States' national average) a study found that for every 10% increase in tree canopy cover there was a 15% decrease in violent crime, and a 14% fall in property crime (theft and arson). See: Gilstad-Hayden, K. et al., "Research note: Greater tree canopy cover is associated with lower rates of both violent and property crime in New Haven, CT", *Landscape and Urban Planning*, Elsevier, 2015; In Philadelphia, an inexpensive project to "green" scrap land led to a 29% fall in gun violence, as well as drops in vandalism and burglaries, in those neighbourhoods. See: Branas, C.C. et al., "Citywide cluster randomized trial to restore blighted vacant land and its effects on violence, crime, and fear", *PNAS*, National Academy of Sciences of the United States of America, 2018.

14   "The Metropolitan Police threaten to take Richard Reynolds into custody": Read all about it: Reynolds, R., *On Guerrilla Gardening*, Bloomsbury, 2009, p.136. Watch it happen: *Guerrilla Gardening, Richard Reynolds*, Bloomsbury Publishing YouTube channel, May 2008, youtube.com/watch?v=L8WTlqiwYdQ

15   "'a form of urban intervention that is broadly accepted and welcomed, *even by those who enforce the law.*'" Millie, A., "Guerrilla gardening as normalised law-breaking: Challenges to land ownership and aesthetic order", *Crime, Media, Culture: An International Journal*, SAGE, 2022. My emphasis.

15   "the role that... ethnicity play[s] in how police treat people": There is a long, well-documented history of institutionalised racism and brutality within police forces. In England and Wales in the year ending March 2021, people from a Black or Black British background were seven times more likely to be stopped and searched, and people from an Asian or Asian British background, or Mixed ethnic background, were approximately two and a half times more likely to be stopped and searched, than those from a white ethnic background. Taken from the "National Stop and Search learning report", IOPC, April 2022.

16   "Incredible Edible co-founder Mary Clear says...": Warhurst, P. and Sikking, A., *INCREDIBLE EDIBLE Seeds to Solutions: The Power of Small Actions*, Incredible Edible C.I.C, 2021, p.15.

16   Caroline Till & Kate Franklin quote: *Our Time On Earth (Exhibition Catalogue)*, Barbican, 2022.

17   "Liz Christy's... community garden": As well as gaining individual legitimacy, Liz Christy's garden – and those created by other green guerrillas, including many by Puerto Rican communities – inspired NYC authorities to set up Operation GreenThumb in 1978, an official initiative that provided cheap leases, supplies, and guidance to community gardeners.

18   "greens grown along train tracks in Mumbai": Elizabeth Soumya, an independent journalist based in India, in conversation with Ellen Miles, July 2022.

18   "crop fields cultivated by landless Kenyan farmers": Leonida Odongo, Kenyan food justice activist, in conversation with Ellen Miles, July 2022.

18   "Brazil's... favela gardens": See: "Brazil's flourishing community gardens", dw.com, April 2022.

18   "food and flowers tended by Syrians in the Domiz refugee camp": Briggs, H., "Seeds of hope: The gardens springing up in refugee camps", bbc.co.uk, May 2018; Dancey-Downs, K., "Planting Seeds in Refugee Camps", regenerosity.world, 2020.

18   "although the... timeline takes place on a Western backdrop, this is more reflective of the way history is written than the movement's true, but hidden, story": It also reflects my personal inability to read histories written in languages other than English.

18   David Tracey quote: Tracey, D., *Guerrilla Gardening: A Manualfesto*, p19.

19   "enslaved farmers ingeniously braided seeds into their hair to retain autonomy, food security, and a connection to the homes they were torn from": Rose, S., "How Enslaved Africans Braided Rice Seeds Into Their Hair & Changed the World", blurredbylines.com, April 2020.

19   "scholar Geri Augusto says...": *Geri Augusto – the importance of okra to enslaved people*, National Museums Liverpool YouTube channel, August 2018, youtu.be/KlGylKHTl4Q; "A green resistance: plants and enslavement", National Museums Liverpool, liverpoolmuseums.org.uk/stories/green-resistance-plants-and-enslavement

19   "As their crops flourished, these brave and bright growers became responsible for the successful presence of rice... and many other species grown in the Americas today": Sousa, E. C. and Raizada, M. N., "Contributions of African Crops to American Culture and Beyond: The Slave Trade and Other Journeys of Resilient Peoples and Crops", *Frontiers in Sustainable Food Systems*, Frontiers, 2020.

19   "In Guantanamo Bay... detainees kept seeds from meals": As American lawyer Peter Sabin Willett summarised, "America denied them seeds and trowels... tried to withhold beauty, but from the grim earth of Guantanamo they scratched a few square meters of garden – with spoons." See: Sabin Willett, P., "Wilting Dreams At Gitmo A Detainee Is Denied A Garden, and Hope", washingtonpost.com, April, 2006.

20   "Nick Hayes says...": In Hayes, N. and Miles, E., "The Road to Common Ground: Trespassing with Nick Hayes". In Miles, E. (ed.), *Nature is a Human Right*, p.158.

20   "'a Common Treasury for All... fed by the Earth'": Winstanley, G., *The True Levellers' Standard Advanced* (1649).

21   "People's Park (California)": peoplespark.org/wp/

21   "[People's Park] was nationally recognised as a Historic Place in 2022": People's Park Committee, "Nationally significant People's Park was officially listed on the National Register of Historic Places on May 24, 2022", peoplespark.org/wp/, May 2022.

21   "the city's visionaries – including... Puerto Rican communities [created gardens]": Pasquali M. et al., *Loisaida: NYC Community Gardens*, A&M Bookstore, 2006.

21 "from 1975–1986, you'd have found the Garden of Eden": The garden was demolished by city authorities in 1986 "out of sheer malice". Lamborn Wilson, P. and Weinberg, B. (eds.), *Avant Gardening: Ecological Struggle in the City & the World*, Autonomedia, 1999, p.8.

21 "Adam Purple": ibid, p.87.

22 "It came to me... public beds": Reynolds, R., *On Guerrilla Gardening*, 2009, p.82.

22 "The global hub...": guerrillagardening.org

22 "enlist", "troop": "troop numbers [are] assigned to volunteers when they enlist at GuerrillaGardening.org" ibid., p.0. "Enlist" was a main menu option on the site.

It is perhaps also worth noting that one celebrated guerrilla gardener told me Reynolds assigned them a "troop number" in his book, without asking to do so.

22 "self-appointed general": "looking down on the 'ranks' from his... self-appointed general's position", McKay, G., *Radical Gardening: Politics, Idealism and Rebellion in the Garden*, Frances Lincoln, 2011, p.189.

PURPOSE (PP.28–51)

31 "Proximity to quality nature is linked to better mental health... and much more": Miles, E., "Welfare", pp. 28–33; Li, Q., "The Secret Power of the Forest: From a Feeling to a Science", pp. 36–48. In: Miles, E. (ed.), *Nature is a Human Right*, 2022.

31 "Around 1 in 3 people in England do not have access to nature near home": A mapping tool used by the government's adviser for the natural environment in England shows around a third of people don't live within 15 minutes' walk of a natural green space. Natural England, "How Natural England's Green Infrastructure Framework can help create better places to live", naturalengland.blog.gov.uk, December 2021.

31 "100 million people in the USA live further than 10 minutes' walk from a park": Chapman, R., "Prioritizing Environmental Justice in Climate Conservation", tpl.org/blog/prioritize-environmental-justice-push-climate-conservation-goals, May 2021.

32 "There are 37 billion acres of land on Earth... the Pope owns 177 million acres.": Cahill K., "Who owns the world?", newstatesman.com, March 2017. Find out more in: Cahill, K. with McMahon, R., *Who Owns the World: The Surprising Truth about Every Piece of Land on the Planet*, Grand Central Publishing, 2010.

32 "Half of England is owned by less than 1% of its population": Shrubsole, G., *Who Owns England?: How We Lost Our Land And How to Take It Back*, William Collins, 2020.

32 "Black people in England are nearly 4 times as likely as white people to have no access to outdoor space at home": Office for National Statistics, "One in eight British households has no garden", ons.gov.uk, May 2020.

34 "wiping out species on Earth at 100 to 1,000 times the natural rate": "[B]irds, mammals and amphibians have been going extinct 100 to 1000 times faster than we would expect. Researchers think this might even be an underestimate." See: Ritchie, H. and Roser, M., "Biodiversity", ourworldindata.org/biodiversity, 2021.

34 "The UK has lost nearly half its biodiversity since the Industrial Revolution": Lai, O., "UK Biodiversity Loss Nearly at 50%, At Risk of 'Ecological Meltdown'", earth.org/uk-biodiversity-loss/, October 2021.

34 "One-third of wildlife in the USA is at risk of extinction": Blackledge, S., "A third of the nation's plants and animals are at risk of extinction", environmentamerica.org, November 2022.

34 "It's estimated that dozens of species go extinct every day, with as many as 30–50% of all species on Earth going extinct by 2050." Ferguson, L., "The Extinction Crisis", now.tufts.edu, May 2019.

36 "@SFinBloom": greenearthgardeners.com/sfinbloom

37 "'One in four native bees in North America are endangered'": Center for Biological Diversity, "Landmark Report: Hundreds of Native Bee Species Sliding Toward Extinction", biologicaldiversity.org, March 2017.

37 "'Sightings of the western monarch butterfly have dropped 99.9% since the 80s'": University of Arizona, "Dramatic decline in western butterfly populations linked to fall warming", sciencedaily.com, March 2021.

40 Ron Finley quote: Ron Finley in conversation with Ellen Miles, September 2022.

40 "seeing beauty around us, compared to desolation or dereliction, has real impact": Broken windows theory says that each unattended problem in a neighbourhood affects people's attitude towards

that area, which in turn leads to greater problems. See: Kelling, G. L. and Wilson, J. Q., "Broken Windows", theatlantic.com, March 1982.

40   "Dr Samantha Walton… tells me": Dr Samantha Walton in conversation with Ellen Miles, August 2022.

40   "Dr Chanuki Illushka Seresinhe and her colleagues… analys[ed] 1.5 million ratings of various outdoor settings": Seresinhe, C., Preis, T. and Moat, H., "Quantifying the Impact of Scenic Environments on Health", *Scientific Reports* 5, Nature Portfolio, 2015.

40   "'Plain grass wasn't so highly rated… there's something about wilder nature that people are innately drawn to'": Dr Chanuki Illushka Seresinhe in conversation with Ellen Miles, 2021.

40   E. O. Wilson quote: Wilson, E. O., *Biophilia*, Harvard University Press, 1984, p.74.

40   "Looking at flourishing plant life can replenish energy… and restore focus": Jo, H., Song, C. and Miyazaki, Y., "Physiological Benefits of Viewing Nature: A Systematic Review of Indoor Experiments", *International Journal of Environmental Research and Public Health*, MDPI, 2019.

40   "People living in 'very scenic' places are more likely to report 'good' or 'very good' health": Researchers cross-referenced census data on citizen-reported health from England and Wales with 1.5 million *Scenic-Or-Not* ratings. The *Scenic-Or-Not* website allows users to rate 217,000 photos (covering nearly 95% of the 1-kilometre/0.6-mile grid squares of Great Britain) out of 10, from "not scenic" to "very scenic". See: Seresinhe, C., Preis, T. and Moat, H., "Quantifying the Impact of Scenic Environments on Health", 2015.

41   "Policymakers point fingers (in the wrong direction)": Rather than make healthy food more accessible, the UK government drafts policies that make HFSS foods more inaccessible, such as banning multi-buy deals on such items. See: Department of Health and Social Care, "Restricting promotions of products high in fat, sugar or salt by location and by volume price: implementation guidance", gov.uk, October 2022.

41   "Food systems and policies… make unhealthy food more accessible (and appealing) than healthy options": In the West, we buy most of our food from multinationals with annual turnover in the tens of billions of US dollars. These organisations are allowed to market their dangerous products (with multi-million-dollar campaigns) without the limitations placed on other unhealthy substances, such as cigarettes and alcohol.

41   "a rise in obesity": In high-income countries, obesity prevalence is highest among the poor. See: Templin, T. et al., "The overweight and obesity transition from the wealthy to the poor in low- and middle-income countries: A survey of household data from 103 countries", *PLoS Medicine*, PLOS, 2019.

41   "a rise in… Type 2 diabetes": Diabetes UK, "Our Reaction to the Spring Statement", diabetes.org.uk, March 2022.

41   "13.5 million households in the USA are in 'food deserts'": The USDA has identified 10% of 65,000 U.S. census tracts – containing 13.5 million households – as food deserts. See: Miller, N. S., "Food insecurity and food deserts in the US: A research roundup and explainer", journalistsresource.org, September 2022; U.S. Department of Agriculture, Food Access Research Atlas, ers.usda.gov/data/fooddesert

41   "In the UK, it costs twice as much to get 100 calories from fresh, single-ingredient food than from ultra-processed, readymade meals": *What Are We Feeding Our Kids?* (BBC One, 2021).

41   "[In the UK] 1 in 5 people's diet consists of 80% preservative-heavy, vitamin-low food": Mangan, L., "What Are We Feeding Our Kids? review – junk food exposé will leave you queasy", theguardian.com, May 2021.

41   "[In the UK] people on the lowest incomes would have to spend nearly 75% of their 'disposable' income on food to achieve the government's healthy eating guidelines": Scott, C., Sutherland, J., and Taylor, A., "Affordability of the UK's Eatwell Guide", The Food Foundation, September 2018, foodfoundation.org.uk/sites/default/files/2021-10/Affordability-of-the-Eatwell-Guide_Final_Web-Version.pdf

41   "In Northern Ireland… to afford healthy food": "NI low-income families need to spend up to half of weekly income to afford a healthy food basket", consumercouncil.org.uk, June 2021.

42   "Guerrilla Graft": I learnt of guerrilla grafting (what it is and how to do it) through the work of San Francisco's Guerrilla Grafters. Find out more about their work at guerrillagrafters.net

44 "Zak Stein": Stein, Z., "If education is not the answer you are asking the wrong question: why it's time to see planetary crises as a species-wide learning opportunity", *Transformative Educational Alliance*, Perspectiva Press, 2019.

44 "Ron Finley thinks…": Ron Finley in conversation with Ellen Miles and Tayshan Hayden-Smith, July 2021.

44 "Children immersed in nature grow up to be more environmentally conscious adults": See: Chawla, L., "Childhood Experiences Associated with Care for the Natural World: A Theoretical Framework for Empirical Results", *Children, Youth and Environments*, University of Cincinnati, 2007; Bird. Dr W., cited in: Moss, S., "Natural Childhood", National Trust Report, 2012.

44 "Being in nature… aids memory and focus": For example, one study found that spending an hour in nature can improve your memory and attention span by 20%. See: Berman, M. G., Jonides, J. and, Kaplan, S., "The Cognitive Benefits of Interacting With Nature", *Psychological Science*, SAGE, 2008.

44 "a 3% increase in urban greenery was linked to a 2.6 point increase in local schoolchildren's IQ": See: Bijnens, E. M. et al., "Residential green space and child intelligence and behavior across urban, suburban, and rural areas in Belgium: A longitudinal birth cohort study of twins", *PLoS Medicine*, PLOS, 2020.

45 "Strong social ties improve health": Social ties improve heart health, brain health, and life expectancy, and also positively influence health behaviours. See: Harvard Medical School, "Making connections good for the heart and soul", Harvard Health Publishing, 2007; Fratiglioni, L. et al., "Influence of social network on occurrence of dementia: a community-based longitudinal study", *The Lancet*, Elsevier, 2000; Holt-Lunstad, J., Smith, T. B., and Layton, J. B., "Social Relationships and Mortality Risk: A Meta-analytic Review", *PLoS Medicine*, PLOS, 2010; Umberson, D. and Montez, J. K., "Social relationships and Health: A Flashpoint for Health Policy", *Journal of Health and Social Behavior*, SAGE, 2010.

45 "Strong social ties… boost happiness": Rohrer, J. M. et al., "Successfully Striving for Happiness: Socially Engaged Pursuits Predict Increases in Life Satisfaction", *Psychological Science*, SAGE, 2018.

45 "In England, those aged 16–24 are the most likely to feel lonely 'often' or 'always'": Department for Digital, Culture, Media & Sport, "Official Statistics: Wellbeing and Loneliness – Community Life Survey 2020/21", gov.uk, July 2021.

45 "In England, those aged 16–24 are the… least likely to feel a strong sense of belonging to their neighbourhood": 56% of younger age groups (16–24 and 25–34) feel strongly that they belong to their immediate neighbourhood. For over 35s it was 65–75%. See: Department for Digital, Culture, Media & Sport, "Official Statistics: Neighbourhood and Community – Community Life Survey 2020/21", gov.uk, July 2021.

45 "disabled people are almost four times more likely than non-disabled people to experience persistent loneliness": 13.3% of disabled people reported feeling lonely "often" or "always", compared to 3.4% of non-disabled people. See: Office for National Statistics, "Disability, well-being and loneliness, UK: 2019", ons.gov.uk, December 2019.

45 "racism, xenophobia, and other forms of discrimination trigger loneliness": Kennedy, L., Field, O., and Barker, K., "Barriers to belonging: An exploration of loneliness among people from Black, Asian and Minority Ethnic backgrounds", British Red Cross and Co-op, 2019.

45 "over a third of homeless service users often feel isolated": Sanders, B. and Brown, B., "'I was all on my own': experiences of loneliness and isolation amongst homeless people", 2015, crisis.org.uk/media/20504/crisis_i_was_all_on_my_own_2016.pdf

45 "we're more likely to return a stranger's dropped glove… in green urban spaces": Guéguen, N. and Stefan, J., "'Green Altruism': Short Immersion in Natural Green Environments and Helping Behavior", *Environment and Behavior*, SAGE, 2014.

45 "we're more likely to… strike up a conversation with someone from another culture… in green urban spaces": Seeland, K., Dübendorfer, S., and Hansmann, R., "Making friends in Zurich's urban forests and parks: The role of public green space for social inclusion of youths from different cultures", *Forest Policy and Economics*, Elsevier, 2009.

45 "we're more likely to… behave selflessly in green urban spaces": Weinstein, N., Przybylski, A. K., and Ryan, R. M., "Can Nature Make Us More Caring? Effects of immersion in Nature on Intrinsic Aspirations and Generosity", *Personality and Social Psychology Bulletin*, SAGE, 2009.

45   "Hafsah Hafeji tells me...": Hafsah Hafeji in conversation with Ellen Miles, September 2022.

46   "the Grenfell Tower disaster": In the early hours of the 14th of June, 2017, a 24-storey council housing block caught alight. Grenfell Tower's cut-price combustible cladding, along with a "litany" of other "serious safety breaches", combined with the fire brigade's "stay put" command, resulted in the tragic loss of 72 human lives. Closing the inquiry into the incident, Richard Millett KC, the inquiry's lead counsel, concluded: "each and every one of the risks... were well known by many... [E]ach and every one of the deaths that occurred in Grenfell Tower on the 14 June 2017 was avoidable."

At the time of writing, the Met police are investigating people for serious criminal offences (including corporate manslaughter and fraud) in relation to the failings that led to this terrible loss of life. Trials may not begin until 2025.

See: Booth, R., Bowcott, O. and Davies, C., "Expert lists litany of serious safety breaches at Grenfell Tower", theguardian.com, June 2018; Apps, P., "Grenfell Inquiry 'able to conclude every death was avoidable' as its lawyer slams ongoing 'merry-go-round' of buck-passing", insidehousing.co.uk, November 2022; Dunne, J., "Grenfell: Met police 'absolutely focused' on criminal probe into blaze", standard.co.uk, June 2022; Booth, R.,"Grenfell fire: focus shifts to possible criminal convictions as inquiry ends", theguardian.com, November 2022.

47   "Maxilla City": maxillacity.org; The building was claimed by resident squatters in the aftermath of the Grenfell tragedy. Tayshan says they've been inspired by Frestonia, a nearby street that became an independent republic in the 1970s. See: Amrani, I., "'This is not a squat' – how the Grenfell community is taking control of its destiny", theguardian.com, December 2017; frestonia.org

48   "Reclaim the Streets [May Day protest, 2000]": "Flower Power Digs At Roots Of Capitalism", squallmagazine.com, May 2000.

48   "Reclaim the Streets... the group who'd bored holes into a motorway and planted trees in them": Reclaim The Streets, London, 1996, M41, rockingthecity YouTube channel, youtube.com/watch?v=OUHY7KwL61o; "M41 Reclaim the Streets", urban75.org

48   "Reclaim the Streets... released a statement": Reclaim The Streets, May Day Press Statement, 2 May 2000.

49   "the scene on the day descended from peaceful celebration into violent chaos": "2000: May Day violence on London streets", news.bbc.co.uk

49   "Chris Wilbert": Wilbert, C., "The Apple Falls From Grace". In: Deep Ecology and Anarchism: A Polemic, Freedom Press, 2017, p.123.

PLACE (PP.52–77)

62   "Rewilding The City": rewildingthecity.com

64   "a children's story called Mary's Meadow": Ewing, J. H., Mary's Meadow (1883–84).

65   "The UK has over 313,000 miles of road verges in rural areas": When rewilded, one mile of flower-rich road verge can produce 20kg (44lb) of nectar sugar per year, enough to feed millions of pollinators. See: Plantlife, "The Good Verge Guide: Your go-to guide for transforming local verges into wildlife havens", plantlife.org.uk/application/files/7916/1191/6240/Road_verge_guide_2021_WEB.pdf

66   "The Garden of Eden Crescent": @sparkingcommunity

70   "Make A Vertical Planter": There are also various ways to add irrigation systems to vertical gardens, but they're a little intimidating for those getting started. If you'd like to look into this, check out: Houseful of Handmade, "DIY Vertical Garden with Drip Watering System", housefulofhandmade.com/diy-vertical-garden-drip-watering-system/

72   "By one calculation...": "[W]e may have already passed the point where concrete outweighs the combined carbon mass of every tree, bush and shrub on the planet." See: Watts, J., "Concrete: the most destructive material on Earth", theguardian.com, February 2019.

72   "Depaving": Depaving can also mean replacing hard surfacing with porous material, such as gravel or woodchip, to allow for rain to drain.

72   "guerrilla planters in... Belfast": Have You Heard About The Wildflower Alleys In The Heart Of Belfast?, RSPB Video YouTube channel, April 2022, youtube.com/watch?v=fNZRwzaifsA&t=9s

74   "About 17% of land in the USA's big cities lies vacant or abandoned": Newman, G. D. et al., "A current inventory of vacant urban land in America", Journal of Urban Design, 21:3, Taylor & Francis, 2016.

74   "10% of the nation's census tracts are identified as food deserts": "The Locator identifies about 10 percent of the approximately 65,000 census tracts in the United States as food deserts. About 13.5 million people in these census tracts have low access to sources of healthful food." See: Wright, A., "Interactive Web Tool Maps Food Deserts, Provides Key Data", usda.gov, April 2021.

74   "In the UK, it's common for allotment waiting lists to be years long": Revealed by a Freedom of Information Act request. See: "These are the Longest Waiting Lists for an Allotment in the UK", myjobquote.co.uk, October 2021.

74   "In the UK… developers buy up plots of land as an investment": Wainwright, O., "Britain has enough land to solve the housing crisis – it's just being hoarded", theguardian.com, January 2017.

77   "Park(ing) Day": myparkingday.org

77   "'a parking space was an incredibly cheap piece of San Francisco real estate'": "Park(ing) Day", johnbela. com/work/parking-day

77   "'The fundamental elements of a good outdoor public space… and a sense of being in nature.'": "Park(ing) Day" (image slideshow), ibid.

PEOPLE (PP.78–97)

83   "Community Groups": You can find community organisations near you through your council website. Go to: gov.uk/find-a-community-support-group-or-organisation

86   "On Sundays… people are more relaxed, friendly, and altruistic": Beyond intuition, I have no evidence to support this! It simply feels self-evident.

88   "Somerford Grows": spacehive.com/somerfordgrows

96   "The Garden of Earthly Delights": gardenearthlydelights.org

PLAN (PP.98–123)

103   "Invasive species": "Most invasive species are neither terribly successful nor very harmful." See: "In defence of invaders", economist.com, December 2015.

103   "Himalayan balsam": Find out more about the threat of its spread: wildlifetrusts.org/wildlife-explorer/wildflowers/himalayan-balsam

103   "'native' versus 'non-native' is becoming an outdated concept": Find out more: Shah, S., "Native Species or Invasive? The Distinction Blurs as the World Warms", e360.yale.edu, January 2020.

114   "The Pansy Project": thepansyproject.com

120   "Around 1 in 5 people in the UK are disabled": Estimates from the Family Resources Survey: financial year 2020 to 2021, indicated that 14.6 million people in the UK had a disability (22% of the total population). See: commonslibrary.parliament. uk/research-briefings/cbp-9602/#:~:text=The%20 latest%20estimates%20from%20 the,period%2C%20up%20from%202018%25

121   "wheelchair-accessible… materials": See: Jay, S., "Wheelchair Accessible Garden Paths: Getting Around", epicgardening.com, March 2022.

121   "ensure there's sufficient contrast between text and backgrounds": Contrast checker: webaim.org/resources/contrastchecker/

122   "Mad About Cork": instagram.com/madaboutcork

PARTS (PP.124–139)

128   "The Subversive Gardener": subversivegardener.com

130   "Recycling Projects in your area that rescue and redistribute items": For instance, in North-East London, Walthamstow's Forest Recycling Project. See: frpuk.org/

134   "Seed Streets Brooklyn": instagram.com/foodbabysoul

137   "multinational chemical companies' monopolisation of the global seed market": "Whereas farmers around the world used to have ownership over the seeds they used, in the 20th century, control was wrested from the hands of millions of individuals by giant biotech and chemical companies. Today, as biologist Tyrone Hayes notes [in *Seed: The Untold Story*], 90% of seeds used to grow food are owned by these international goliaths. See: Miles, E. and Fagborun, T., "'Africa is being recolonised': Seed sovereignty as a form of resistance", shado-mag. com, March 2022.

137   "a way to safeguard seed diversity – which is essential to future-proof food and ecosystems": A Growing Culture (AGC) and Gevaerd, S., "What is seed sovereignty?", shado-mag.com, March

2022; 94% of the world's seed diversity has vanished in the last century; See: Betz, J. and Siegel, T. (dirs.), *Seed: The Untold Story*, (Collective Eye Films, 2016).

PLANTING (PP.140–159)

144   "peatlands are vital... carbon stores": Peatlands play a vital role in mitigating climate change: the world's peatlands store twice as much carbon as its forests. See: unep.org/news-and-stories/story/peatlands-store-twice-much-carbon-all-worlds-forests

145   "'No Dig' planting": Find out more at charlesdowding.co.uk/start-here/

146   "Green & Blue Eco Care": greenandblueecocare.wixsite.com/gbec

152   "Avoid planting too deeply, or in too narrow a hole: 90% of all young tree deaths are attributable to these mistakes": Royal Horticultural Society, *RHS How To Garden: A Practical Introduction to Gardening* (New Edition), DK, 2021, p.197.

154   "The Garden Classroom": thegardenclassroom.org.uk

154   "'Islington has the lowest amount of open access green space per person in England'": Islington is the most densely populated local authority area in England and Wales, with 15,517 people per square km, meaning it has the smallest amount of green space per head of population. Only 13% of the borough's land is green space, the second lowest proportion of any local authority in the country. See: islington.gov.uk/~/media/sharepoint-lists/public-records/communications/publicity/publicconsultation/20192020/20200326islingtonbiodiversityactionplan2020to2025web1.pdf

155   "the Fibonacci sequence": The Fibonacci sequence is a series of numbers, starting with 1, in which each number is the sum of the two that come before it: 1, 1, 2, 3, 5, 8, 13, 21... and so on. The ratio of each number to the next (1.618), known as "the Golden Ratio", creates inherently aesthetically pleasing compositions. Various plants follow the Fibonacci sequence and Golden Ratio in a number of ways, from the number of leaves around a stem, to the spiral of a rose's petals. Find out more here: thejoyofplants.co.uk/fibonacci-numbers-science-plants

PROTECT (PP.160–173)

162   "Whatever the time of year, there's always gardening that can be done": See: Spence, I., *RHS Gardening Through the Year: Month-by-month planning, instructions and inspiration* (New Edition), DK, 2018.

163   "we shouldn't be making cities greener because some people have hayfever": The evidence actually suggests that hayfever has worsened as society has urbanised (with the resulting rise in temperatures, and atmospheric CO_2), with distressed plants having to increase their pollen rate to survive as a species, along with pollution exacerbating hayfever symptoms.

Natasha Hinde of Huff Post UK reports: "There's also been a 'significant increase' in the number of those with the allergy [hayfever]... Allergy UK suggests the increase may be closely linked to rising temperatures... Amena Warner, head of clinical services, says... 'Studies show plants produce more pollen as a response to high atmospheric levels of CO_2...'" See: Hinde, N., "Hay Fever Has Definitely Got Worse, You're Not Imagining It", huffingtonpost.co.uk, April 2021.

166   "From petitions to sit-ins, there's a wealth of tactics to consider": For a wealth of tried-and-tested tactics, I recommend everyone read climate activist Noga Levy-Rapoport's essay, "Rebel With a Cause: How to Become an Activist". In: Miles, E. (ed.), *Nature is a Human Right*, 2022, pp.243–257.

167   "commonly used herbicides... [harm] bees". Carrington, D., "Glyphosate weedkiller damages wild bee colonies, study reveals", theguardian.com, June 2022; Weidenmüller, A. et al., "Glyphosate impairs collective thermoregulation in bumblebees", *Science*, AAAS, 2022.

167   "commonly used herbicides... [harm] humans": "Can weed killers containing glyphosate cause cancer?", medicalnewstoday.com/articles/does-roundup-cause-cancer; "Can Roundup cause cancer?", deohs.washington.edu/edge/blog/can-roundup-cause-cancer; pan-uk.org/health-effects-of-pesticides/

168   "The Ron Finley Project": ronfinley.com

170   "99% of the time, they'll be kind, curious folk": This is not only my personal experience: goodness is the default human nature. Don't believe me? Read: Bregman, R. *Humankind: A Hopeful History*, Bloomsbury Publishing, 2020.

INDEX

PICTURE CREDITS

The publisher would like to thank the following for their kind permission to reproduce their photographs:

(Key: a-above; b-below/bottom; c-centre; f-far; l-left; r-right; t-top)

14 **Alet Pretorius / Daily Maverick.** 20 **Photograph © Harvey Wang.** 27 **Ellen Miles** (b). **Ottawa Guerrilla Gardening Club** (cr). 34 **SFinBloom.art.** 35 **SFinBloom.art.** 36 **SFinBloom.art.** 37 **SFinBloom.art** (tl, r). 39 **SFinBloom.art** (r). 40 **Ellen Miles.** 43 **Tom Levy** (tr). **@SparkingCommunity** (tl). 44 **@SparkingCommunity.** 48-49 **Alamy Stock Photo: Rob Lacey** (tc). 49 **Paul Harfleet** (b). 55 **Melynda Gierard** (t). **Ellen Miles** (bl). 56 **Ellen Miles** (b). 57 **Ellen Miles.** 58 **Héctor García** - Bestselling author of *A Geek in Japan and Ikigai: The Japanese Secret to a Long and Happy Life*: (b). **Ellen Miles** (t). 59 **Melynda Gierard.** 60 **Mad About Cork.** 61 **Ellen Miles** (b). 62 **John Welsh.** 63 **John Welsh.** 65 **@SparkingCommunity** (bl, br). 67 **@SparkingCommunity** (tl, tr). 68 **Melynda Gierard.** 69 **Getty Images / iStock: Oksana Aksenova** (b). **Aisling Patton** (t). 72 **Dreamstime.com: Frans Blok** (l). 73 **Elaine Hill** (br). **Mad About Cork** (tr). **Ottawa Guerrilla Gardening Club** (bl). 74 **Garden of Earthy Delights.** 75 **Camille Gazeau** (br). 77 **Getty Images Stan Honda / AFP** (tr); **Justin Sullivan** (tl). 81 **Mad About Cork** (tl, bl), **Ellen Miles** (r). 82 **Ottawa Guerrilla Gardening Club** (b). 85 **Ellen Miles.** 87 **@GreenAnd BlueEcoCare.** 89 **Somerford Grows** (crb). 91 **SFinBloom.art** (bl). 92 **Ellen Miles.** 94 **Ellen Miles.** 101 **Ellen Miles.** 107 **Alamy Stock Photo: Susan E. Degginger** (crb, cb). **Getty Images / iStock: Drew Beynon #DBPic** (clb). 112 **Ellen Miles.** 114 **Paul Harfleet.** 115 **Photo by Wen Chi-Su** (tr). **Paul Harfleet** (cr). 116 **Ellen Miles.** 117 **Somerford Grows.** 119 **Ellen Miles** (t). 120 **Mad About Cork** (tr). **Ellen Miles** (b). 122 **Mad About Cork** (b). 123 **Mad About Cork** (tl). 126 **Ellen Miles** (cr). 128 **Vanessa Harden** (crb). 129 **Vanessa Harden** (crb). **Roel Paredaens** (tl). **Sitraka Rakotoniaina** (tr). 131 **Melynda Gierard** (br). **Ellen Miles** (r). 134 **Melynda Gierard.** 135 **Melynda Gierard** (tr). **Poppy Carnation:** (tl). 136 **Ellen Miles.** 143 **Ellen Miles.** 144 **Ellen Miles** (t). 145 **Ellen Miles.** 146 **@GreenAnd BlueEco Care.** 147 **@GreenAndBlue EcoCare** (tl, tr). 151 **Ellen Miles.** 157 **Ellen Miles** (l, r). 164 **Mad About Cork** (bc). 165 **Ellen Miles.** 168 **The Ron Finley Project.** 169 **Ellen Miles** (r). **The Ron Finley Project** (tl). 172 **@GreenAnd BlueEcoCare** (tr). **Ellen Miles** (bc). **Ottawa Guerrilla Gardening Club** (br). **@SparkingCommunity** (cla, bl).

All other images © Francis Augusto

ACKNOWLEDGEMENTS

A huge, heartfelt thank you to everyone who helped bring this book into the world.

First and foremost, thank you to all the guerrilla gardeners who shared their personal stories and photographs for this compendium: the people bursting from these pages – including the wonderful Alan, Domi, Grace, John, Kate, Lizzy, Marnie, Melynda, Paul, Peter, Phoenix, Robin, Ron, Ruth, Seng, Shalaco, Simone, Sulekha, Tassia, Tayshan, and Vanessa – and other brilliant folk who wished to remain anonymous.

To Frank Starling, Shzr Ee Tan, and Nikita Montlake for their thoughtful sensitivity reads. To Chanuki, Elizabeth, Hafsah, Jenny, Leonida, and Samantha for their expertise on vital topics. To the friends and family (Kit, Lucy, Nikita, Roger, Rosie, and Sophie) who read some early drafts. And to the DK team for pulling strings and spinning plates behind the scenes.

Thank you to the immensely talented artists who brought everything to life: Francis Augusto for his warm, candid photographs (and great company); Bess Daly for smashing the layout design (and generally being a rockstar); Lauren Martin for the joyful cover illustration; Nick Shepherd for the "How-tos", and Tania Gomes, who brilliantly wove these creative forces of nature together. Thanks also to Rafi Spangenthal for the original Dream Green "blobs".

An endless, depthless thanks to my editor Krissy in particular, who expertly captained this project without ever losing her calm or good humour (though if you don't consider puns "good humour", we'd both lost it from the get-go).

Last but not least, I'm grateful to all the Dream Green crew, especially Aleja, Livvy, Matt, Vaughan, and Will. And to all the other patient friends who've stood in the rain as I pile moss into a wet bag, or crouched beside me on a dusty roadside clutching a makeshift gardening fork. There'll be more to come in future, so for that I can only thank you in advance.

ABOUT THE AUTHOR

Ellen Miles roots for nature in urban neighbourhoods. She writes, speaks, and consults on our need for nature, and how progressive policy can fulfil it. In 2020, she founded the Nature is a Human Right campaign and in 2021 launched Dream Green, a social enterprise that helps people get guerrilla gardening. Her activism has reached millions worldwide, through TikTok (@OctaviaChill) and international press.

"An amazing urban environmentalist who is greening up abandoned lots and corners in the city, spreading wildflower seeds and caring about the ecology of grey cityscapes."
Hila "The Killa" Perry

"Miles is sowing the seeds of guerrilla gardening much further than Hackney."
The Big Issue

"ELLEN MILES... HAS SPARKED A WHOLE NEW GENERATION OF GUERRILLA GARDENERS."
RTÉ 2

Senior Editor Sophie Blackman
Senior Designer Tania Gomes
Editorial Director Cara Armstrong
Senior Production Editor Tony Phipps
Senior Production Controller Stephanie McConnell
**Jacket and Sales Materials Coordinator/
Publishing Assistant** Jasmin Lennie
Editorial Manager Ruth O'Rourke
Design Manager Marianne Markham
Art Director Maxine Pedliham
Publishing Director Katie Cowan

Designers Bess Daly and George Saad
Editor Krissy Mallett
US Editor Sharon Lucas
US Consultant John Tullock
Proofreader Alice McKeever
Legal readers Victoria Simon-Shore and
Nicola Evans
Sensitivity readers Frank Starling and Shzr Tan
Indexer Ruth Ellis
Illustrators Nick Shepherd and Lauren Martin
Photographer Francis Augusto

The publishers would like to thank Victoria Simon-Shore and Nicola Evans for the legal read, Frank Starling and Shzr Tan for the sensitivity read, Alice McKeever for the proofread, and Ruth Ellis for the index.

First published in Great Britain in 2023 by
Dorling Kindersley Limited
DK, One Embassy Gardens, 8 Viaduct Gardens,
London, SW11 7BW

The authorised representative in the EEA is
Dorling Kindersley Verlag GmbH. Arnulfstr. 124,
80636 Munich, Germany

Copyright © 2023 Dorling Kindersley Limited
A Penguin Random House Company
10 9 8 7 6 5 4 3 2 1
001–333484–Jun/2023

A CIP catalogue record for this book
is available from the British Library.
ISBN: 978-0-2415-9334-9

Printed and bound in Slovakia

For the curious

www.dk.com

MIX
Paper | Supporting
responsible forestry
FSC™ C018179

This book was made with Forest
Stewardship Council™ certified
paper – one small step in DK's
commitment to a sustainable future.
For more information go to
www.dk.com/our-green-pledge